FLEE

9 TO 5

Get **6–7 figures**

~ AND DO ~

what you love

FLEE 9 TO 5

Get 6–7 figures AND DO *what you love*

BEN ANGEL

WILEY

First published in 2014 by John Wiley & Sons Australia, Ltd
42 McDougall St, Milton Qld 4064

Office also in Melbourne

Typeset in 11/13.5 pt ITC Giovanni Std Book

© Dare 2 Be Central Pty Ltd

The moral rights of the author have been asserted

National Library of Australia Cataloguing-in-Publication data:

Author:	Angel, Ben, author.
Title:	Flee 9 to 5, Get 6–7 Figures and Do What You Love/ Ben Angel.
ISBN:	9780730307006 (pbk)
	9780730307020 (ebook)
Notes:	Includes index.
Subjects:	Success in business.
	Marketing.
	Business planning.
	Self-actualization (Psychology).
Dewey Number:	650.1

Cover design by Xou Creative, www.xou.com.au

Cover image: iStockphoto.com/Photomorphic

Author photo taken by Kon Iatrou of Ikon Images, www.ikonimages.com.au

Printed by Ligare Pty Ltd

10 9 8 7 6 5 4 3 2 1

Disclaimer

CONTENTS

ABOUT THE AUTHOR

 Ben Angel, author of the books *CLICK—The New Science of Influence* and *Sleeping Your Way to The Top in Business*, is Australia's leading personal branding and marketing authority. With an international fan base over 35000 strong, Ben has worked with the likes of Toyota and Australia Post, and has helped many other top celebrity brands find the tipping point in their careers and companies, and dramatically increase their profiles and profits. You can regularly catch Ben in the media commenting on everything from politics, music and business to careers and lifestyle. Visit www.benangel.com.au for more.

ACKNOWLEDGEMENTS

This book is the result of a hurricane and a 20-second meeting with the dynamic Matt Holt, from Wiley in the US. Thanks Matt. Whatever I said to you in that 20-second conversation, please text it to me — I was jet-lagged!

Secondly, thanks to one of my best friends, Alex Moloney, for being by my side as we rode out the storm together. I promise never to buy you a cinnamon-scented candle for any birthday, Christmas or random gift EVER, and to not travel during hurricane season again. I couldn't have got through it without you.

To Kristen Hammond, whom I've had the amazing pleasure of working with at Wiley. Your support, encouragement and belief in me as an author have been nothing short of humbling. None of this would have been possible without your support and the incredible team at Wiley to make this book possible.

A big shout-out and much love to two special people — my mum, Fay Angel, for being a rock in my life and inspiring me to step up my game; and my dad, Steele Angel, for being a constant presence in my life, despite no longer being here with us in physical form. I could never have asked for a better upbringing and two better role models.

To my amazing friends, whom I consider family, Johnny, Mat, Dean, Jaya, Nick, John H, Adam, Rosie, Paul, Mike, Neil and Daniel. And, a special mention to the gorgeous Andrea Moss of *The Real Housewives of Melbourne*. You've all impacted my life in ways that you'll never truly understand. I could not be more grateful for having each of you in my life.

And, most importantly, my thanks to you the reader. Without you, I'd be ordinary. You make me strive to be more of who I am. This book is dedicated to each and every one of you.

INTRODUCTION

Have you ever had a burning desire to flee the 9 to 5 and finally do what you love and get what you want? Are you sick of making peanuts by sharing your knowledge with your employer, who makes millions from it and pays you a tenth of what it's worth, just because you've been conditioned to believe that there's no other way? And did you know that you can get paid six to seven figures a year by sharing your knowledge, expertise and stories with those who can benefit from your experiences (no matter what your subject or industry) *and* help transform lives and shape the world we live in?

It may seem far-fetched, particularly if you believe that no one would pay to listen to your advice... and your friends typically tune out when you chime in. But the reality is there are tens of thousands of individuals all around you doing just that right now. They're finally getting paid what they're worth and gaining the respect they deserve. They're the new breed of celebrity entrepreneur, known as *agents of influence*.

You'll see them working away on their laptops while sipping on their soy mocha lattes in Starbucks. They're online providing how-to advice to help other people transform their lives and businesses, travelling the world experiencing different cultures and making money on autopilot, while everyone else around them drowns under an ocean of work, debt and stress.

They are agents of influence and agents of change, the entrepreneurial masters of the new information and social media age who are making millions, average people who have become influential experts, authors, speakers, coaches and online entrepreneurs. They don't feel like they do a day's work in their lives because they are doing what they love and love what they are doing.

They are people just like you and me, but they have taken a simple yet profound step to change their lives by packaging their skills, stories and experiences into marketable products that solve problems that keep others up at night.

They're finding solutions to everything from how to flourish in life, relationships, career and business; to challenges in whatever other subject they are passionate about. They are generating books, articles, blogs, online courses, audios and DVDs that are quick and cheap to create and make them millions.

No matter what your skillset, there are people willing to pay you for that knowledge to help shape their lives and businesses, so you can finally profit from what you love doing.

Every single day millions of people are searching Google and social media channels for answers to their burning questions — questions they could be paying you to answer. Even if you don't fully believe it right now, with your knowledge and expertise you hold the key to helping them. Whether or not you consider yourself an expert, you know things that others don't, and in the new world economy that knowledge is bankable.

There is a bigger need than ever before for information that helps others become leaders in their respective fields. They need mentoring, guidance and advice to help them get started or get ahead of the game, and they are looking for individuals like you, who have been there and done that, to help them.

If you are already an author, speaker, coach or entrepreneur, you will probably get what I'm saying immediately. You need to make your messages more marketable and massively profitable by taking creative and innovative approaches to get your message out to millions cost-effectively. Or you may have picked up this book because you know that you were meant to help others succeed, and you know that *you* will succeed by doing so.

It doesn't matter what stage of the game you're at — whether you're in full play or just getting started. In this life-changing book I'll share with you practical, step-by-step, advanced strategies to design, finetune and market your knowledge and expertise in ways that are not only profitable but inspirational. These strategies will help you create a life that frees you to flee 9 to 5, make a six- or seven-figure income, do what you love and get what you want.

This book is your invitation to join the agents of influence and benefit from the new information and social media economies that are at your fingertips. Join me now, for we're about to go on an adventure together — beginning in one of the harshest and most vibrant cities in the world ...

1 IT ALL STARTS HERE
'If you can make it in New York, baby, you can make it…'

→ How to turn your knowledge and expertise into profits

Your time is limited, so don't waste it living someone else's life.
— **Steve Jobs**

It was an assault on all my senses.

Jet-lagged and almost delirious after the long flight from Australia, I found myself in Times Square, in the heart of New York City, with 35 kilos of luggage in tow and no idea where I was staying.

It had just turned 9 pm on a Saturday night in October 2012, and the crowds were teeming under the bright city lights, as they do night after night. P. Diddy gazed down from a skyscraper-high billboard, flaunting his latest eau de toilette — that's French for 'I don't give a damn'. I had more immediate things to worry about than smelling great, like getting on the Net and locating my accommodation for the next four weeks in a city I'd never been to before.

After 22 hours breathing in the fug of other people's air (and, dare I say, other vapours), I was disoriented, and the lights were blinding. My business partner at the time had given me the general location of where I was to stay, but the idea was that on my arrival I'd check my email ... and voilà, I'd look up and be right there.

But my phone wouldn't connect ... and that's when things quickly unravelled.

Into the vortex

Being new to the city, I was convinced I was going to get mugged. Clearly the two painful minutes of *Law & Order* I once watched were too much. That annoying sound they play at the start of every episode was on repeat in my head. According to IMDb.com, it 'was created by combining close to a dozen sounds, including that of a group of monks stamping on a floor'. *Keep it down, monks!*

After dragging my luggage around for a couple of hours, hauling it out of the countless subway grates that lined every street, while I searched for a wifi connection, I finally found a Starbucks.

It was packed, with a lineup like you'd find at a Justin Bieber concert. I stood outside and attempted to connect through the glass.

What I didn't know then was that a little over a week later I'd find myself back in front of the very same Starbucks, on the same mission, but by then joined by many other visitors and New Yorkers looking for new accommodation after Hurricane Sandy had come barrelling down on the city. *Great!*

After ten minutes of trying I finally got a signal. I opened my email ... to find that my accommodation had been cancelled in transit. *Aaghh!* Thankfully my (now ex) business partner had booked me in somewhere else, but only for one night.

You see, in two days' time I was booked to pitch to more than 70 of the world's top TV and radio producers. During my four-week stay I would conduct media interviews, sell truckloads of books and online products, shape the world we live in and then make my way back to Australia with a smile on my face after a massively successful media campaign. Not.

You know when things just don't go to plan?

You try to create a tipping point in your life and career, and however hard you try destiny has a different plan for you at that moment in time. And you get sucked up into this vortex that won't let you go. It could be a job, a relationship, or office cubicle walls that seem to be constantly closing in on you. You get paid peanuts to share your expertise and knowledge and it goes completely unappreciated and unnoticed. In fact, your stapler gets more attention than you do, and it's probably handled better too.

I had been sucked up into a vortex of massive proportions — and not in a good way! I was working my butt off 24/7 and wasn't being rewarded for it. Just before leaving for NYC, I'd come off an Australian speaking tour in which I'd spent more than eight hours on stage in all of the major cities over the course of two weeks, entertaining and educating. It's hard staying perky on stage when you've had only a few hours of broken sleep!

I was exhausted … and now, within less than 72 hours, I had to find a place to stay, print off all of my media material and prepare for a series of pitches — all with a big smile on my face, while fighting through some serious jetlag — along with keeping my business running and making money back home.

I felt like my eyes were going to roll back in my head at any second and I'd slow-motion fall onto my arse, *Matrix* style, at the most inopportune time.

I was at a key point in my life when I had to make some serious decisions.

These included:

- Was I going to continue down a path that clearly wasn't rewarding me financially or emotionally? I was constantly exhausted and was ageing horribly! The cash flow question was always knocking on the back door of my mind, and it was getting louder and louder.

- How was I going to dramatically increase my income and decrease my debt, both of which tasks seemed completely impossible within the required time frame?

- And when was I going to grow a pair and finally do what I wanted to do: make an impact on this world; create the legacy only I could; make more money; travel; have more fun; and hop, skip and jump right off this treadmill without falling on my face?

Can you relate?

I've known from the age of ten that I was meant for something bigger than I knew was possible at the time. I just didn't know what. I knew I was meant to impact others' lives in ways that were emotionally rewarding for me and life changing for them. I wanted to share my stories and experiences with the world to help shape it in my own unique way with my own unique ability.

Maybe you've had a life-changing experience in business or life that you would love to share with others — an experience, or knowledge and expertise, that could have a profound impact on other people's lives, by solving a problem they have been struggling with for years, or making it easier for them in some way or another in business, career, love or life.

Or maybe you're a business or life coach, social media expert, personal trainer, health practitioner, psychologist, marketer, publicist, chiropractor, graphic designer, photographer, stylist, designer, copywriter, spiritual healer, project manager, architect, personal assistant, human resources manager, virtual assistant or organiser, website developer ... or you're in sales.

Whatever your area of expertise or newfound interest, without a shadow of a doubt you already know in your heart of hearts that being an agent of influence and change, an author, speaker, coach, consultant or entrepreneur, is a path to creating meaning within your own and others' lives. A person who shapes others' opinions and empowers them to make better decisions in their lives because of the experience and knowledge you bring to the table.

I know you have skills, tools, strategies and techniques that could transform lives and inspire change in others on a global scale, and you have your own distinct take on it.

But how can you have this profound impact in the world when now the very idea seems unfathomable? How can you share your own stories, experiences, knowledge and expertise with the world in a way that has real reach and meaning? And how do you find your own confident voice and create a platform from which you can successfully package, market and monetise your message?

Turning your knowledge and expertise into profits: why my story is critical to your success

For years I was in the 'expert' business. I started out as an accredited life coach and then transitioned to business coaching, engaging with various mentors along the way while adding layer upon layer to my skillset, including personal branding, marketing, social media, publicity, business growth and styling. I learned by putting my money where my mouth was. I didn't go to university. I entered the school of hard knocks.

I set my own curriculum based on the life I wanted to lead and my creative yearning to keep pushing myself further.

But with no real mentors to look up to and to model how I could market and monetise my message and share my stories and techniques in a profitable and automated way, I became incredibly frustrated.

I'd spent so much time helping my clients make millions when I could have been doing that myself. I was sick and tired of making other people money at my own expense. I knew I could be doing things a lot smarter with a lot less stress and a much bigger payoff. I could develop the flexibility and freedom to choose when I wanted to work and on what.

Does this sound familiar?

My clients' results weren't run of the mill, and they still aren't today ... One of them became a best-selling author; another pulled in an extra $300 000 in revenue within the first three months; another took their database from 200 new opt-ins per week to more than 2000 *per week*, worth hundreds of thousands of dollars in added revenue; for another I helped secure international media coverage, from *Vogue* to *CLEO* to major newspapers and online blogs all around the world, turning an unknown brand into one the world was suddenly following with bated breath.

But there was a problem. *Their success was coming at my expense.*

We're all great at what we do and most of us work our tails off to get results for others — at what always seems like a cost to our own success. For me, it was a matter of prioritising. My success had to rival or better that of my clients. The mantra 'Their success is your success' is only relevant when helping others isn't sending you broke!

And that was what was happening to me. I'd landed in New York City, ready to share my expertise and knowledge and finally make some serious money, when everything fell to pieces ... later to be reborn in a new and more profitable way.

New York was my catalyst for change — what's yours?

It only took a hurricane and a series of unfortunate events to create a serious tipping point in my life. That tipping point sparked something magnificent.

The total transformation took less than six months and included selling online digital products worth more than $100 000, paying off $50 000 in debt that the business had accrued due to poor management, taking back full control of the business and reinventing it from the bottom up, securing an expert role on a new TV show called *Manscape* that aired six times a week, and landing a cameo role on *The Real Housewives of Melbourne* (part of the massively successful reality TV franchise from Arena).

Within a few short months I'd turned a struggling business into one that was suddenly pulling in six figures — without employing a massive team to do it.

And that was only the start...

So what happened in those six months that made such a profound difference to my life, my income and the way I thought about making money? It was simple. I had worked out the formula to turn my knowledge and expertise into profits.

I found a way that worked for me, my lifestyle and my clients that was profitable, exciting and rewarding, simply by leveraging, packaging, marketing and monetising what I already knew into books and products that sold online on autopilot. It's an approach that can work for anyone, in any industry for any product or service — and yes, that includes you, even if you are starting from scratch!

But before I delve into how you can dramatically transform your life, let's just stop for a minute and think about the way you're living right now.

Is it time to reinvent your life?

I mean, really think about it. Could your life be better? Could you be making more money and doing more of what you love? Could you be experiencing greater recognition and having a greater impact that has true meaning for you and for others?

If you're currently feeling the way I did — that is, that you're making your clients or employer richer than you through your expertise and knowledge — and if you're ready to change your life and embark on an extraordinary journey, and you want to do it quickly, as I did (without making the same mistakes I made), read this book closely.

As we share this journey together I'll reveal to you lessons that will fundamentally shift the way you think about the story you have to share with the world, how you make money and how you spend your time.

I will share with you my own journey of fleeing 9 to 5, a struggling business and overwhelming debt to get paid five figures monthly and to build a business on autopilot that has the potential to make millions within a year.

This book will not only show you how to do it, but will show you how to leverage your time, money and resources to free you up to travel where and when you want and to create the life that you want to live.

I'll share with you my journey to New York and how it changed my life, and how it could relate to your future as an 'agent of influence and change' in the company of the new rich who have fled the rat race.

I have more than ten years' experience working with thousands of businesses in industries as diverse as beauty, automotive, expert, wellbeing, pharmaceuticals, celebrity and fashion, among others. As you'll soon discover, my journey wasn't always an easy one. Unlike other books out there, I won't try to sell you unrealistic ideas or create unrealistic expectations of how you can be successful with next to no effort. What I will do, however, is step you through the quickest and most honest route to profiting from your expertise and knowledge and creating new and unbelievable opportunities for yourself.

Together we will focus on three fundamental points of view:

- *We are each here to shape the world we live in* — on both a local and a global scale, whether you believe it right now or not. The best and most profound and leveraged way to do this is by sharing your knowledge and expertise (on any topic of interest in any field) in a way that reaches out to the rest of the world.

- *We are each gifted with a story that relates how we came to be who we are today* — and the various factors that shaped this journey. This journey has very real market value and importance to others.

- *We can be paid incredibly well for sharing our message and story with the rest of the world* — helping people to reach their goals while at the same time building a profitable business and having a true impact on thousands, even millions, of others, especially on our home turf.

Ideas, development, production, distribution and growth: the winning sequence

Behind this mask there is more than just flesh. Beneath this mask there is an idea ... and ideas are bulletproof.
— Alan Moore, *V for Vendetta*

As you dive deeper into these pages, you'll uncover a logical and clear sequence of steps to creating, marketing and launching products that package your expertise and knowledge. I'll take you through various exercises to help you define your life's mission, from uncovering your idea and developing, producing and distributing it, to finally profiting from it and growing an online or offline business that has the potential to yield you millions.

To make the most out of this process, here are three powerful tips to multiply and magnify your results:

- *Use a notebook to capture your ideas.* Inspiration can strike at any time and you need to be able to capture these ideas quickly. I recommend the online notebook Evernote, available for Mac or Android (because you may like to set up a lifestyle in which you get to travel to cool and exotic places). You want easy access to your information, ideas, plans and strategies on the go. Securing your ideas will help you take control of the process and lay a solid foundation for future success, no matter what your plans might be. Sync it on your laptop, mobile phone and other devices so you can make notes and develop ideas on the move, no matter where you are.

- *Complete the recommended exercises.* I'll be asking you to complete exercises to get some real skin in the game so you can begin your journey today. Set aside some time each day so it becomes a daily routine — a ritual that will truly help you create a life you only ever imagined.

- *Planning vs completion.* It is my experience that 95 per cent of your time initially will go into the planning and research phases rather than the actual delivery and completion phases. Trust the process and the process will support you.

It doesn't matter what industry you work in, what your specialty is or what product or service you want to create and sell, I will inspire you and guide you through the entire process. And I'll introduce you to powerful techniques to carry you through those times when it doesn't feel so great or you hit a bump in the road.

How will turning your knowledge and expertise into profits get you there?

That's what I'm here for. It all begins with you and the reason you're here — the unique outlook you have to offer the world. It's an outlook that has evolved through your upbringing and education, whether formal, through university, or in the school of hard knocks like me — all the years of experience and the energy and time you've put into building up your knowledge and expertise.

It's shaped by the reasons why you do what you do, and it's uniquely yours. You own the delivery, the style and the personal brand that goes with it — all the bankable elements that move beyond the knowledge and skills you possess and allow you to separate yourself from other experts within your current industry or one you're about to enter as a brand-new start-up business.

---

*Share your story and advice, and be a part of this
billion-dollar industry*

It's not just about your skillset either. Our world is built on stories, and stories generate outcomes. Turn on your smart phone, TV or computer now to see what I mean. Whether you're logged into Facebook or Twitter, listening to music, watching YouTube, Googling for how-to advice, reading a book or watching a movie, the one common denominator that connects all of these platforms is the story the content shares with the audience. Content that is designed to educate, entertain and inspire.

Music, web and print all belong to this billion-dollar industry, and with the huge amount of content being uploaded to the Net daily it's easy for us to believe we've reached a new stage in the information age — excess. The massively popular blogging site Tumblr now hosts more than 100 million blogs, with an average of 72 million blog posts being added every single day. That's a lot of people wanting to share their opinions and 'how-to' advice, and yet only a tiny fraction of them make serious money, or even any at all.

Why? This new age we've entered has created a new economy that few yet have a handle on. They simply don't know how to monetise the intangible asset — knowledge, the world's most valuable resource.

Any question or problem you need answering has a solution online, which means either:

- you won't make any money because others already have it covered, or
- you must find a way to be part of the top 1 to 2 per cent of people who know how.

Business, career, love and life: what people are really paying for

People are overloaded with information but what they haven't worked out is how to consolidate it using a logical sequence of steps that will help them achieve specific outcomes — from finding a partner, building their wealth, growing their business, advancing their career, managing their team or becoming an effective leader, right through to losing weight, learning how to knit or getting rid of nits!

Every day millions of online searches are performed by individuals ready to buy solutions that will help them advance in one of the four major profit categories that today's agents of influence and change are tapping into: *business, career, love* and *life*.

Millions of consumers are seeking practical, step-by-step how-to advice that will transform their lives and help them reach their desired outcomes in these categories, and in each there are profitable niches within profitable niches. When you extract this magic and package it up into marketable products such as books, DVDs, online courses, audio programs, articles and blogs that people can experience and enjoy, you'll be able to transform your life in three crucial ways:

Maximise your time and resources

If you find yourself on repeat, sharing the same information over and over again, it's time to create a product or service that you can sell on autopilot. This allows for greater flexibility in where you work, how you work and what you work on. As I write this I find myself in a funky little Melbourne coffee shop with the smell of freshly ground coffee beans wafting through the air and the buzz of customers all around me. With my laptop, I can work in a cafe, on a plane, on a beach or in my home office. In fact, I did three trips to New Zealand while writing this book — and still making money online. Why don't I have a formal office? Why would I waste time commuting every day when I could spend it socialising, keeping fit or working on projects I love?

Part of my first book, *Sleeping Your Way to The Top in Business* (for a free copy, visit www.benangel.com.au), was written on Ko Phi Phi Don in Thailand, the island opposite Ko Phi Phi Leh, where the movie *The Beach* was filmed, while sipping on banana daiquiris and taking in the breathtaking view of crystal-blue water. Did someone say it was happy hour?

Monetise your knowledge and expertise

One of the biggest traps in life is trading time for money. Trading one-to-one, instead of one-to-many, means you'll find yourself forever on the treadmill at the mercy of everyone else's schedule instead of defining your own. When you are well positioned within your market with a well-defined product offering, you gain credibility, which you can turn into a bankable personal brand with the capacity to generate income for years to come with little effort.

Once this brand is successfully established you'll find that opportunities suddenly appear from unexpected directions, such as TV, radio, newspapers, speaking opportunities and high-paid consulting work, all of which can propel your business to a tipping point that will see its value spiral upwards.

Simplify your life

Selling one-to-many, or leveraging, frees you from the need to answer countless emails or waste your time in meeting after meeting. It takes the headache out of business and life when systems are put in place that free you to focus on other exciting projects or simply to take more time out for yourself and your family. Achieving this is not a complicated process; you need only employ a specific sequence of strategies to attain your goal.

When you discover how to create a business that supports your lifestyle you'll find that suddenly things shift in every area of your life, and you'll begin to see things in a completely new light. Why? Because you'll be making a difference in other people's lives too, and there isn't a feeling in the world to beat that.

Tips and resources

→ You can reinvent your life and create a profitable business by leveraging, packaging, marketing and monetising your own unique knowledge and expertise.

→ By marketing your particular skillset, and with the application of certain tools, strategies and techniques, you can transform lives and inspire change in others on a global scale.

→ Leverage your time, money and resources to free you up to travel and to create the life that you want to live.

For a free copy of my first book, *Sleeping Your Way to The Top in Business*, visit www.benangel.com.au.

---

2 VISION
The agents of influence

→ The few, the remarkable, the vision...
and the millions

The empires of the future are empires of the mind.
— **Winston Churchill**

Creating a vision is essential if you want to flee 9 to 5, get paid a six- to seven-figure income and do what you love. That creation is born here.

Melbourne, Australia, 6 pm — waiting with bated breath. I had my finger hovering over the 'record' button. I was just minutes away from speaking with a former Oprah producer who was preparing me for my time in New York, and I was ready to absorb every word.

What would she say? How would I need to position myself? What did I need clarity on to really make this work? Most importantly, how would I stand out from all of the other experts who were attending the conference…beyond my Aussie accent that Americans thought was hot! Thanks, Hugh Jackman!

These were just a few of the thoughts racing around my head on a dirt bike, muddying up my clarity. But, before I could take the call, I had to make a few critical decisions…because the real work had just begun.

I knew there were only two ways I could make the most out of this brief encounter:

- *I could look past the impossible.* I was completely out of my comfort zone. The trip to New York was just one of many steps I'd laid out for myself to help monetise my message. The mere fact that I was being coached by a former Oprah (and Grammy award–winning) producer persuaded me that anything was possible. I had to open myself to a grander vision. A vision that took my breath away, even if it did still seem out of reach at that stage.

- *I could create the remarkable.* To overcome any hurdles I might encounter on the journey, I had to know precisely what I wanted for myself and for others, and to know intuitively who I was going to 'become' in taking this giant leap forward. All while allowing myself enough flexibility to grow into it. In essence, I had to create a remarkable vision for myself—to be different, to become an agent of influence, someone with a limitless vision of what life could offer.

Agents of influence

Agents of influence are individuals whose expertise and knowledge within a specialised field is highly valued, sought after and rewarded. Their ability to sway people's opinions and transform lives places them at the heart of the conversation in their niche. The respect they have won affords them the flexibility to 'do what feels right'. People are swept up by their vision not only of themselves but of others. This influence is intoxicating but, more profoundly, life changing.

Million-dollar personal brands—how their vision makes them wealthy

Flick on the TV, open a newspaper or walk into a bookstore, and you will soon encounter these agents of influence. There's Tony Robbins, Suzie Ormond, Tim Ferriss, Dr Phil, Marie Forleo, Abraham Hicks, Bethenny Frankel, Robert Kiyosaki and thousands of other high-profile personal brands who have made fortunes from the particular vision they hold of themselves. They achieved this level of success by monetising their messages into on- and offline products, consulting services, speaking engagements, webinars, TV appearances, endorsement deals and more.

So why is it, then, that we need your voice?

It's simple. Like their competitors before them, none of these agents has the one thing that you have: your unique perspective, education, experience and vision. Nor do they have your unique personality.

You are a 'limited edition'.

The only thing that businesses and companies can't copy is the essence of who you are. When you bring this essence to the fore, competitors may attempt to copy you, but they never quite can. It's simply not sustainable or authentic.

In my first book, *Sleeping Your Way to The Top in Business*, I wrote, 'Personal branding is self-expression amplified to influence and command attention'. The experts you see out there have packaged themselves into marketable products that people flock to, invest in and buy from because they've amplified *who* they are, rather than hiding it from the world. They themselves are their most marketable asset.

This doesn't mean they are necessarily the best in the world, but their marketing has established how they are perceived. In this book I will teach you how to do the same in the most leveraged and effective way possible, so that within a few short months you can become a first-class expert while finally doing what you love.

Most critically, there is a simple principle that must guide all agents of influence:

No single person has all of the answers.

Phew! Breathe that in for a minute and really digest it. Your input could transform an entire industry simply by looking at an old problem from a new perspective, taking a fresh approach. You don't have to know all the answers. You just need to know answers to the specific problems you aim to solve — problems that you are most likely already an expert on and solving right now in your day-to-day life. One well-known example of an agent of influence who completely turned her life around is Bethenny Frankel.

Bethenny Frankel — broke to $100 million dollar deal

Your starting point could be rock bottom ... and even then you're still ahead of the pack!

Bethenny Frankel was on the brink of financial collapse before being cast for *The Real Housewives of New York City*. She soon shot to stardom and has become one of the most successful stars in the Arena franchise, with best-selling books, workout DVDs, a Skinnygirl drink empire that sold for $100 million and a talk show produced by Ellen DeGeneres's company. Not only has she capitalised on turning her expertise in and knowledge of health and lifestyle into marketable information products that sell on- and offline to create residual income, but she's also turned it into physical products via the Skinnygirl range — a natural extension of her core message of living life well.

Her unapologetic outgoing personality, combined with the connection she created with her audience via TV, books, social media and DVDs worked towards establishing an international brand worth millions. She created the connection that birthed the company she has today, and she started it all with next to nothing.

Giants levelling the playing field: why now's a perfect time to get started

The great news is that the playing field has been levelled and paved for you, as it was for Bethenny, to begin right now, no matter what your starting point.

You don't need to hire staff, you don't need a physical shop front and you don't need tens of thousands of dollars in your bank account to get started — nor do you need prior knowledge of creating products, marketing or business, for that matter. And you don't need to be an extrovert, as many believe, or to catch a break on a reality TV show.

I've had no formal training in any of these areas, and for a guy who grew up on a cattle and cropping farm in country South Australia, who started with zero budget but went on to build an online following of more than 35 000, I know what's possible. More importantly, through painstaking testing and measuring over ten years I know how to help you reach your goals, and to figure out what works and what doesn't, and where you should invest your time and energy in getting started in the lucrative expert industry.

The six fundamental principles of lifestyle design

Everything you can imagine is real.
— **Pablo Picasso**

As an agent of influence in training, or even as a pro who is seeking to hit the next rung of success, you're creating a vision. Every day. With every thought.

This vision must create dramatic tension between where you are and where you want to be in order for it to be propelled into existence. To do this we begin by answering several key questions in the categories of *see, do, create, experience, inspire* and *share*, which are the six fundamental principles of lifestyle design. Agents of influence begin their journey by designing their ultimate life; the business is then designed to fit around this. So let's begin.

1. See

What do you see yourself doing and/or having in six to 12 months? If you could do or have anything you wanted within this time period, and you knew that anything was possible, what would it be? Using the templates on the following pages, get clear on what your future lifestyle looks like. This is the vision that will compel you to make profound changes in your life that you never thought were possible.

Neale Donald Walsch writes, 'Life begins at the end of your comfort zone'. Get uncomfortable in this exercise and move beyond your existing comfort level. Each expansion of your comfort zone brings about an expansion of you—your lifestyle, your wealth and, most importantly, your potential.

You'll look back and realise that it was the accumulation of small steps over time that was really what you needed all along. For example, I used to watch many reality TV shows on Arena and picture myself in one. I didn't know how. I just knew what I wanted. Six short months later I received a phone call inviting me to make a cameo appearance. How it happens for you is not important. What is important is that you have the vision to see further than you see right now.

2. Do

What do you see yourself doing on a weekly basis? There's nothing more frustrating than seeing someone who doesn't understand what they're capable of, given time. I came face to face with this myself recently. Landing an advisory role with the talented New Zealand fashion designer Annah Stretton, I soon realised I was selling myself short. This phenomenal woman will fly from Auckland to China to source fabrics and tour the factories, then to Brisbane to speak at various women's events, then on to Melbourne to look at possible stores, meet with me and attend a show, then back to Auckland — all within the space of a week. She'll be back at work the next day as if she'd popped down the street to grab a cup of coffee.

Imagine what you could do if your thinking was limitless? Imagine what you could do if you had all the money, time and energy in the world? How would you be spending your weeks? What would you be doing? Where would you be travelling? What would you be working on? We all have the same allocation of time each day; it's how we decide to use it that's crucial.

3. Create

What kind of lifestyle would you like to create? Lifestyle creation is an art and, like an artist, you must choose the palette you wish to paint with. With an abundance of colours and contrasting experiences to choose from, for many it can become an overwhelming experience. Set your fears and worries aside. Worry detracts from your experience of today and creates a vacuum that attracts more of the same. It wastes energy and time that could be better spent on creating a lifestyle that enriches your life daily.

Let go of your inhibitions, judgements, fears and worries and begin to paint. What kind of lifestyle do you yearn for? Perhaps one that includes financial abundance, freedom to travel to exotic countries, time to give back to charities, greater connection with your family. How would you spend your time? Create it freely.

4. Experience

What would you like to experience on a monthly basis? Experience is the gift of life. After all, what are we really living for other than to experience a rich variety of interactions and events over the course of our time on this planet? To enrich this experience we must be strong-willed and clear on what these experiences are to be. Go to your local travel agent and grab as many brochures as you can. Jump online and look at what you'd love to experience more of, whether travelling, adventure, shopping, education, love, connection or self-expansion. Now's not the time to hold back.

5. Inspire

What is inspiring you to make this change in your life or those of others? To be successful in life, we must understand the *why*. Why did you decide to make the change now and, critically, *what* inspired you to make the change? Did you have your own New York moment when you just knew that enough was enough? Did you help someone solve a problem and just know you had to share the solution with the rest of the world?

Know your why *and the* how *will present itself.*

---

6. Share

Sharing your story and message is the secret to creating a lifestyle business that can generate long-term profits. What is the story or message you would like to share with the world? Did you experience crippling pain that turned you to yoga, so that now you'd like to teach others via DVDs and books? Did you help a business grow by six or seven figures by implementing your strategies, and you'd love to create an online course that better leverages your time and increases your income? Did you have a life-changing experience that you'd like to share via an audio program that sells on autopilot? Your story is what will connect you to your audience and them to you. It's what sets you apart from everyone else in your industry. What is your story?

The Lifestyle Design Blueprint

The 15-minute Lifestyle Design Blueprint is a tool that will help you refine and reinvigorate your life by working on the six fundamental principles I've just outlined.

Find yourself a quiet space in which you can let your imagination run wild. Now is not the time to hold back. Don't worry just yet about how your vision can be brought to fruition — we'll get to that later. Get excited and let go; most importantly, whenever you find yourself getting stuck, simply ask yourself, 'If I could be, do or have anything, what else do I want for my life and for those of others?'.

To help you get started, table 2.1 shows a sample blueprint.

Table 2.1: the Lifestyle Design Blueprint (*example*)

See	Do	Create
What do you see yourself doing/having in ____ months? ■ Writing a book ■ Selling online products ■ Travelling ■ Appearing on TV as an expert ■ Speaking at events	What do you see yourself doing on a weekly basis? ■ Learning ■ Writing ■ Meeting with clients ■ Spending time with family ■ Spending time with friends ■ Taking singing lessons	What kind of lifestyle would you like to create? ■ Financial abundance ■ Flexibility to work when I want ■ Freedom to travel ■ Time for hobbies
Experience	**Inspire**	**Share**
What would you like to experience on a monthly basis? ■ Travel ■ Shopping ■ Charity work ■ Further education	What is inspiring you to make this change in your life or those of others? ■ Personal experience ■ Expertise in my field ■ Fulfilling a passion ■ Creating a legacy	What is the story you would like to share with the world? ■ It's possible to flee 9 to 5. ■ We each have a calling. ■ The steps to do it are: _____ _____ _____

Visit www.benangel.com.au/flee9-5 for a printable copy of this template.

Now it's your turn. Use table 2.2 to complete the template for yourself. Jump into this task with abandon and, whatever you do, don't edit your own life. You only get one shot at it — live it well and create it freely.

Table 2.2: the Lifestyle Design Blueprint (*your turn*)

See	Do	Create
What do you see yourself doing/having in ____ months?	What do you see yourself doing on a weekly basis?	What kind of lifestyle would you like to create?
■	■	■
■	■	■
■	■	■
■	■	■
■	■	■
■	■	■
■		

Experience	Inspire	Share
What would you like to experience on a monthly basis?	What is inspiring you to make this change in your life or those of others?	What is the story you would like to share with the world?
■	■	■
■	■	■
■	■	■
■	■	■

Extracting the essence and bottling the passion: the key to your happiness

The happiness of a man in this life does not consist in the absence but in the mastery of his passions.
— **Alfred Lord Tennyson**

These questions are designed to extract the essence of your passion, the most potent resource you have as a human being.

When we connect with this passion, 9 to 5 no longer factors in. You could work 24/7 and be happier than Kim Kardashian with a brand-new sponsorship deal. It's got zero to do with the hours you work and everything to do with whether or not you are doing what you love.

Money doesn't come before you do what you love — it comes as a result of it.

By homing in on your passions now, you uncover the fundamentals for creating a profitable business and fulfilling lifestyle.

I want you to really think about the answers you just entered in the Lifestyle Design Blueprint. Picture them, smell them, feel them and hear them and, most importantly, experience them. Create an online dream board using Evernote by copying and pasting images of how you see your life to come. Sync it to your phone and look at it every night before you go to bed. Make this part of your daily ritual because, as we know, all successful individuals follow daily rituals that support their development.

Your answers to these simple yet powerful questions will underpin everything you do now and in the future, and will fast become the driving force that compels you to keep going when times get tough, when you lose flow, when you get frustrated, when expectations aren't met and you're greeted with brick wall after brick wall and filled with self-doubt. You will draw your inspiration and motivation from these answers, which will shape not only your world but eventually the world *we* live in.

Which brings us to a critical question.

What kind of agent are you?

Potential career paths were lost on me as a kid. I had no idea what I wanted to do, how to find out or where to get started. I just knew that I valued experience and contribution over a title I could hang on the wall. I tried everything, including writing music, management, investing in a personal development company, training as a travel agent, running a speed-dating business. (Did it help get me dates? No!) You name it, I tried it. I did everything I possibly could to fit myself into a confined box, not realising that there were options available to me based on my skillset at the time — I just didn't know how to package and market them successfully.

This experience helped me devise an easy formula that you can use to instantly uncover your talents, find your strengths and secure your future. My EKP Solution (see table 2.3, overleaf) breaks down into three easy steps that you can use to identify your current expertise and knowledge (or what you would like to discover), and how to transform that expertise and knowledge into marketable products.

This tool can be used by anyone in any industry, no matter what their area of expertise or specialty. Take a personal trainer, for example, who like many of us trades time for money. Here's an illustration of how such a professional might reimagine their business to increase sales, reduce the need for those 5 am wake-up calls, and create greater flexibility that allows for travel and growth.

Table 2.3: the EKP Solution (*example*)

Expertise	Knowledge
List the precise expertise you possess currently that you would like to focus on or specialise in. ■ Weight loss ■ Motivation ■ Persistence ■ Fitness	What specific outcomes can be achieved via the application of this expertise? ■ How to lose 7 kg in 7 days ■ How to lose baby weight ■ How to get fit in 30 days or less ■ How to increase energy ×10

Products
If you could turn this knowledge into online products that leveraged your time and resources, what formats (e.g. audio, digital download, DVD, video tutorial, online course, webinar series) would you be interested in? ■ 'How to Lose 7 kg in 7 Days' — 60-minute audio program ■ 'How to Lose That Baby Weight' — online video tutorial ■ 'How to Get Fit in 30 Days or Less' — audio and digital manual ■ 'How to Increase Energy ×10' — book

As you can see from the sample above, we focus on three core areas in a simple way to extract and define both your knowledge and how it could be turned into information products that could be sold online.

Now it's your turn to apply this template to your area of expertise. The key is to be as specific as possible when it comes to *how* your knowledge can be applied. If you're looking to enter an entirely new industry, under 'expertise' simply list the skills you are most passionate about learning and developing. This will form the starting point for your 'Quick Start Guide'.

If you're already in the game and doing what you love, but you'd like to make it more profitable, by completing this exercise you'll uncover other products that could be added to your marketing mix to increase your income with little effort.

Now complete the template below in table 2.4.

Table 2.4: the EKP Solution (*your turn*)

Expertise	Knowledge
List the precise expertise you possess now that you would like to focus on or specialise in. ■ ■ ■ ■	What specific outcomes can be achieved via the application of this expertise? ■ How to _____ ■ How to _____ ■ How to _____ ■ How to _____

Products
If you could turn this knowledge into online products that leveraged your time and resources, what formats (e.g. audio, digital download, DVD, video tutorial, online course, webinar series) would you be interested in? ■ ■ ■ ■

Finding velocity: three archetypes for becoming a successful agent of influence

'Hello?'

'Hello, is this Ben?' asked Danette, the former Oprah producer. 'Are you ready to get started?'

'Absolutely', I replied.

'Then let's begin. It's time for you to take the next big step.'

Does earning a great income and having flexibility in your life sound good to you? Let's make it even better by speeding up the process of helping you find your position in the marketplace by taking a look at the three archetypes for becoming a successful agent of influence.

Following on from the exercises you have just completed, these archetypes are the ultimate differentiators to set you apart from everyone else in your industry. They are designed to get you thinking about how you could be positioned in the marketplace to gain greater traction, sooner.

Polarising

There is nothing more powerful in marketing and life than using your ability to polarise your audience by being unapologetic about who you are. Polarising is the art of creating 'friends and foes' — people who love you and others who absolutely hate you. For many people this idea is frightening. The most important thing to realise is that any expert who enters a new marketplace must create what I call 'industry disturbance'. When your opinions differ from others' in your field you suddenly create fans who will follow your every move and buy from you time after time. Your detractors serve only to amplify your message, and in many cases become the catalyst by which you reach your tipping point for success in your industry. So don't just identify your expertise and knowledge; identify what makes you, through your opinions and personality, different from others in your industry.

Mission

Anyone with a story and a message to share makes it their mission to get people to give a damn about it. In my brief interaction with Danette, the most remarkable takeaway for me was that there is power in simplicity when pitching for a mass audience. It sounds easy, but it's not. It's in the process of subtraction and not addition that we command influence and authority and become formidable communicators. In stripping back who we are, we allow others to strip back who they are.

This creates a connection that instantly separates you from the wannabes, allowing your story and message to shine through.

Don't fall into the trap of thinking that more is more.

Fail fast, fail early, fail often

Perfectionism is the number one enemy of state. As Theodore Roosevelt said, 'It is hard to fail, but it is worse never to have tried to succeed'. Failure is one of the greatest gifts we could ever be given. By failing fast, failing early and failing often, you'll quickly speed up your rate of success and create brand-new stories and experiences that can also be packaged into marketable products.

Lifestyle, vision, expertise and knowledge are key cornerstone concepts. By defining yours you will position yourself for success and create a blueprint for getting anything you want. It is through this clarity that new doors will open and new opportunities flood through. You have just taken the handbrake off your life.

Mid-air jitters

'Thank God!' I thought to myself. I was finally on my way. I'd made it through LAX security. Those guys are scary. I now had to race across the Los Angeles airport in search of my connecting flight. My comfort zone was about to be obliterated and reshaped in a way I'd never experienced.

And something magical was about to happen. In the midst of all the chaos I didn't realise I'd finally cracked the code to the agent of influence's bank account and that within four weeks it would add five figures to my bottom line. And I was about to come face to face with Hurricane Sandy.

Tips and resources

→ Successful agents of influence have a powerful vision of themselves and have packaged themselves into marketable products.

→ Sharing your story and message is the secret to creating a lifestyle business that can generate long-term profits.

→ By homing in on your passions and vision now, you uncover the fundamentals for creating a profitable business and fulfilling lifestyle.

Visit www.benangel.com.au/flee9-5 for printable copies of the Lifesyle Design Blueprint and EKP Solution templates.

3 MONETISATION
Monetising your message

→ How to generate six to seven figures by hacking
the agent of influence's bank account

> *The city seen from the Queensboro Bridge is always the city
> seen for the first time, in its first wild promise of all the
> mystery and the beauty in the world.*
> — **F. Scott Fitzgerald**, *The Great Gatsby*

New York City, 2 am. Seven hours and counting.

It was the morning of the launch of the National Publicity Summit. The lights from Times Square reflected down a corridor of skyscrapers and bathed me in light in my thirty-sixth-floor hotel room on 37th Street, just around the corner from Hell's Kitchen. I couldn't sleep. Jet lag had kicked in and I was angry and frustrated—because tomorrow, well, it was showtime.

In a few hours I was due to meet TV producers, journalists and editors from the likes of *The View*, *Good Morning America*, *Today*, *Time* magazine, *Fast Company* and 70 other influential media reps.

Only problem was, I was on track to attending the function comatose. This wasn't how I'd pictured my trip going at all. Hell's Kitchen was living up to its name.

Being the adventurous type, I had booked through Airbnb, where you rent out a room in someone else's apartment. I wanted to live with real New Yorkers, to experience the city in a way only a New Yorker could.

Big mistake!

Not only did my accommodation cancel on my first night in the city, but this was the best I could find at short notice, before I was locked away in a conference for four full days. There was no time to shop around. My room had floor-to-ceiling windows, no blinds, a bed with slats that would randomly fall off during the night, and no quilt—I used the blanket from the plane!

At 2 in the morning, sitting in the only chair in the room, I decided to work until I fell asleep. I started by writing a promotional email to my database, launching an online product I'd recently created in my spare time. I wasn't sure how it would go. I'd spent only an hour a day over the course of a month on it. I hit Send, rubbed my tired eyes and went back to bed.

Hacking the agent's bank account

The greatest artists like Dylan, Picasso and Newton risked failure.
And if we want to be great, we've got to risk it too.
— **Steve Jobs**

I'd finally done it. I'd hacked the agent's bank account! The product I'd launched at 2 in the morning in New York brought in more than $20 000 in sales that month alone. Finally I was making a serious return on investment with minimal effort, while being in another country!

My business no longer required my 24-hour input. In fact, I'd been unintentionally hindering my own progress by acting on the flawed premise that 'the harder you work, the more you're worth'. But it wasn't about working harder; it was about working smarter and applying the Pareto Principle. Named after economist Vilfredo Pareto, this principle argues that there is an unequal relationship between inputs and outputs, such that 20 per cent of our efforts are responsible for 80 per cent of our results. Now I knew that working out the 20 per cent of my efforts was what I needed to focus on to continue to hack the agent's bank account.

And it all began with ascending.

Ascend your way to profits

As you read through these pages your vision for your ultimate lifestyle business will keep evolving. Increasingly you will gain insights into your own potential to impact the world in a more meaningful way through your knowledge and expertise. And your business's potential to generate repeat business that will drive profit margins higher and higher with each evolution.

Ascending your way to profits begins by persuading your customers of their higher needs.

Because my goal is to help you shape the world we live in, in relation to any industry and any product or service, I want you to focus on ongoing customer transformations, and on contributing to them in numerous ways. Think about how you can help them, not once or twice but three times or more, through a suite of products.

What I call the 'ascension marketing model' is about producing and crafting complementary products or services that continue to help your clients progress to higher levels of experience.

Creating a suite of products is like getting paid compound interest.

Think of it like the school system. We start off in prep school, move on to primary school, high school and then university. Each level of education provides a higher degree of detail and complexity than the one that preceded it. If we were to attend all levels at once, our minds would collapse under the weight of the information. The graduated system creates a seamless experience, presenting information in chunk-size pieces and building knowledge at each level, thereby minimising the chances of becoming overwhelmed and failing.

Business is no different. Ideally every successful business has a defined product and/or service offering that includes lower priced, entry-level products, as well as successively more expensive, sophisticated offerings of greater and more intensive experiences.

Picture Apple Computers. One of many ways Apple has drawn millions of new customers to its products over the years is via the music download program iTunes, available for PC and Mac, which allows users to buy and download music and to manage their collection with a few keystrokes. Apple literally put their shopfront in their customers' hands. But of course it didn't end there. Suddenly iPods was being sold in their millions, soon to be followed by the iPhone and iPad tablets, and users were syncing their music between multiple Apple devices.

This meant that instead of a customer purchasing just one device, they ended up spending thousands on a suite of synced products that needed to be constantly updated, which significantly increased the average dollar spend per customer, not to mention Apple's profits.

This created what is called the 'long tail', the economic concept explaining how the collective demand for less popular items can exceed demand for all of the most popular items added together. iTunes, for example, can carry a huge range of digital music because these digital products have no inventory limitations.

If you like to work on your laptop from a tropical island or a Manhattan coffee shop, then there is really only one way to go when it comes to selling your products, and that's digital. Forget inventory concerns. With digital you never sell out, delivery is automated and you can find cost-effective virtual staff to troubleshoot any customer queries with ease. You remain in control, yet you are ever further removed from the day-to-day chores of running a business. And what I like even more is that the results are immediate. You don't have to wait for a monthly report. You can even set up mobile-phone alerts to notify you each time you make a sale.

The ascension marketing model (AMM)

Work through a sample product offering for your ascension marketing model — to step your customers through the process, from opting into your database via a complimentary offer right through to purchasing your most expensive offering.

Each product created must pre-sell the next: step 1 will build the need for step 2, which builds the need for step 3 ... and so on, just like the school system previously outlined. This technique, called *seeding*, is practised by every successful business. It is the process of implanting a suggestion that there is more to experience — that if you liked that, you'll love this.

It's one of the least pushy ways to sell online, and one of the most respected. You *guide* your customers through your sales process, instead of trying to *force* them through, as many do.

As with the school analogy, this creates a seamless customer experience by feeding information to the prospect or customer in increments, thereby minimising the potential for them to become overwhelmed and fail to purchase.

What do your customers need to get them to the next level, then the level after that?

To put you on the fast track, you can think about this model as having three distinct levels.

1 *Introductory products.* These are free or low-priced digital products with high value, created to form a bond with your target market. They could take the form of a free report, a sample audio, an ebook or a short email course valued at up to $30. This step draws the prospect by way of a digital handshake and is your primary opportunity to demonstrate your knowledge and expertise in a way that makes them

want to find out more about what you have to offer. A mix of free and cheap is crucial, not only to build your list quickly, but to offer something with a low barrier to entry.

2 *Principal products.* Your principal products are set at a higher price point than the introductory products. They could be of similar formats to the ones in step 1, but with a higher level of information or detail. These can be priced between $97 outright and a monthly membership fee at a lower price point (for example, 12 payments of $37.95 — cancel any time). We aim for prices under the $100 mark to increase conversions and once again lower the barrier to entry. Think audio programs, online courses, digital book packs and memberships. You're now providing a higher level of 'how-to' and practical advice.

3 *Forward-looking products.* These are high-end, sophisticated products or services typically involving a higher number of touch points with the customer. Think university-level experience. Whereas in step 2 of the ascension model you gave them a valuable 'piece' of the system, here you offer the complete system with all of the finer detail. Your forward-looking products are your 'secret sauce' recipes — available only to those who perceive the value in them. They can be priced anywhere between $500 and $10 000 plus and include multimedia learning, one-on-one consulting, templates, workshops, webinars, speaking engagements and more.

In each phase you're solving a very specific piece of your customer's problem. You're meeting them at the level of experience or current education they possess on your topic, and helping them to ascend to where they want to be.

As you can see, there are three or more potential steps each prospect could take in relation to your business. Instead of them spending only a little with you by buying one product or service, some customers will have spent well over $5000 by journey's end.

By using this model, your ability to dramatically increase your revenue, reach and free time jumps immediately. Does it take time to create each product/service offering? Yes. Once the products are completed, however, you need only fill your sales funnel and let your automated marketing and sales processes do the work for you.

35 000+ downloads, six figures and counting

In 2012 I decided to do the unthinkable. After the release of my successful first book, *Sleeping Your Way to The Top in Business*, which yielded over $100 000 in sales, I quickly made a digital version free to the public. More than 35 000 downloads and 18 000 weekly email subscribers later, it had added six figures to my business within the first 12 months. A book that had been on the market since 2009 suddenly breathed new life into my business and brand.

It formed step 1 in my ascension marketing model and created a tipping point in my business that helped to attract the attention of TV producers, magazines and newspapers — and, more importantly, new clients.

The great news is you don't need a massive database to get started.

You just need imagination!

It's not rocket science, but it does follow a formula: the AMM template

Imagination is more important than knowledge.
—Albert Einstein

Whether you are at the very start of your journey, your products are a work-in-progress or they are ready to go, in the previous chapter you will have identified the types of outcomes your expertise and knowledge can achieve and the kinds of problems they can solve, and you will have brainstormed some possible product ideas.

To help you take it further, keeping your product ideas in mind, it's now time to put them in a specific order based on the AMM template (table 3.1, overleaf).

Don't worry about how you will create the products just yet, or even how many you will create. We'll get to that in the coming chapters. Use this as a brainstorming session to further refine a marketing model that could help you generate six to seven figures from your expertise and knowledge.

Table 3.1: the ascension marketing model template

Ascension marketing model		
1 Introductory product: (e.g. free book or audio download, email course, report)	Idea #1: _____	Price #1: _____
	Idea #2: _____	Price #2: _____
	Idea #3: _____	Price #3: _____
Price range: (free–$30 maximum)		
2 Primary product: (e.g. online course, audio program, monthly membership club, email course, digital manifesto)	Idea #1: _____	Price #1: _____
	Idea #2: _____	Price #2: _____
Price range: ($97 maximum or monthly fee at lower rate — e.g. $47/week for 3 weeks)	Idea #3: _____	Price #3: _____
3 Forward-looking product: (e.g. complete 'how-to' system, multimedia learning, one-to-one consulting, templates, paid speaking engagements, endorsement/ sponsorship deals, high-end webinars)	Idea #1: _____	Price #1: _____
	Idea #2: _____	Price #2: _____
Price range: ($500–$10 000-plus)	Idea #3: _____	Price #3: _____

Payday prediction and creation costs

Don't spend a cent until you've read this. Here I'll take you behind the scenes to show you a real-life example of one of my products in order to demonstrate key considerations before you spend a cent creating one of your own. This will provide you with valuable insight to help you decide whether or not your idea will fly.

My step-by-step Instant Publicity Marketing System has helped my clients secure international media coverage, from *The Huffington Post*, *Vogue*, *CLEO* and *Marie Claire*, to countless other magazines, blogs, newspapers and radio stations. Its components include:

1 Audio introduction (60 minutes)
   - Creation cost: $0 (recorded using iTalk app on iPhone)
   - Development time: 1 week part-time

2 Instant Publicity Marketing System Guide (100 pages, including templates and samples)
   - Creation cost: $700 for a copywriter to polish content already written.
   - Development time: 4 weeks part-time

3 Media list bonus
   - Creation cost: $500 for virtual assistant team to research names and lists
   - Development time: 3 weeks

4 Online video sales page
   - Creation cost: $100 to hire high-quality video camera for a day; $300 for graphic designer to design online sales page
   - Development time: 3 days

Total initial investment: $1600

Retail: $97 per download

Creation time: 4 weeks

To recoup initial investment: 16.5 unit sales

Some readers may feel the initial development costs are high, and they may not have the finances to fund it, but it's critical to recognise what's possible when you're willing to think differently. For example, I negotiated 30-day billing terms with both the copywriter and graphic designer. This meant that I could take pre-orders for the product prior to launch to secure the funds needed to create it *before* I had to cover my initial start-up costs. You could even crowdfund your product to fund its release using sites such as www.kickstarter.com.

He crowdfunded his way to $287 342

On 18 June 2012 best-selling author Seth Godin launched a Kickstarter campaign for his new book *The Icarus Deception*. After just three hours he had reached his goal of raising $40 000 to demonstrate to his publisher, the bookstores and anyone with a book worth writing that it's possible to start a project using a crowdfunding site.

By the close of his campaign he had secured 4242 backers and $287 342 in pledges. Now, although Seth has a major following, it goes to show that it is possible to have zero funds in your account and yet raise what is needed to get your first product off the ground — as long as you have a solid concept.

I decided to launch this product to my existing list to reduce costs. It generated $30 000 in sales within the first two months, and my online video sales page achieved a 4.4 per cent conversion rate from visitor to buyer, 2.1 per cent higher than the online industry average of just 2.3 per cent. This resulted in an initial profit of $28 400.

What this means is that if you want to make 10 sales a day to generate $970 in daily revenue for a product that retails at $97 per unit, you will need approximately 435 people to visit your site every day — fewer if your conversion rate is higher.

I call this the *2.3 per cent rule*, and use it as my litmus test when working out the viability and potential profitability of new products.

We then need to factor in how much it is going to cost to acquire this traffic.

The method behind my metrics: the #1 secret to unlocking six to seven figures in sales

To be successful, the first thing you need to do is get your head around what needs to be measured and why these metrics are critical to your success. Don't roll your eyes. It's not hard, but you must do this. If you don't, you could go bankrupt! That sounds harsh, but it's true, and that's certainly not the Flee 9 to 5 lifestyle goal.

Here are the three key steps you will need to pay attention to as we journey through this process together:

1 Offline prospecting activity
   - number of new leads
   - new customers
   - sales revenue
   - response rate
   - conversion
   - return on investment (ROI).

2 Online marketing
   - website traffic
   - opt-ins via key landing pages
   - opt-in percentage
   - shopping cart conversion
   - numbers of orders
   - ROI based on your average visitor value.

3 Email activity
   - click-through rate
   - bounce rate
   - list size
   - list growth
   - list conversion.

Don't feel overwhelmed by this level of detail. It will all become clear by the end of the book, by which time you'll know exactly what's required to become successful.

Ultimately you are spending time and money on email campaigns or buying traffic with a view to bringing people to your site and converting them into clients. How much is it costing you now to perform each activity, and what is your return on your investment? It might be costing you $30 for each new visitor, but how will you know if that is too expensive? You need to measure it against your *average visitor value* and your profit margins. Then you'll know whether you are getting value for money.

To work out your average visitor value, follow these steps:

1 Write down the number of sales you have made for the week (for example, 10 units).

2 Multiply this by the value of the transaction (for example, $100).

3 This equals your total revenue ($1000).

4 Divide it by the number of unique visitors to your site (for example, 1000).

5   Your average visitor value in this example would be $1.

Using this example, your campaign is costing you $30 for an average visitor value of $1, which means you're losing $29 in advertising costs each time someone visits your website. This example isn't designed to shock you, but simply to show you how important it is to keep an eye on the numbers.

No list, no worries: how to get started without a database to market to

If you don't have a list of prospective customers, a Facebook following or a fan base ready to buy what you have to sell, don't worry. To launch a product successfully you don't need any of them, but what you do need are several highly targeted places in which you can purchase this exposure.

With a Facebook or Google AdWords campaign, for example, you can set your daily marketing budget as low as you like — $20, $50, $100-plus — depending on your objective. This will require a little, critically important, research on your part. But, compared with the $30 per new customer in the previous example, you can spend as little as 10 cents on Facebook and under $1 on Google.

Reverse engineering

So far in this book I have stepped you through how to uncover your talents and expertise. Now it's time to find a market to match it and to assess its viability. I call this process *reverse engineering*. Instead of trying to contort yourself into something you're not, we start with *you*, because we want the business to be built around your particular expertise. This is very significant when it comes to marketing yourself and your products.

To get started, you need an idea of the potential size of your customer base to see how you can compete with others in the marketplace. For example, let's take Facebook advertising. To be successful on Facebook you must be very clear about who your target market is.

The ability to determine a business's ideal prospects lies at the heart of its success, although it's never truly given the attention it deserves. This key activity is at the core of what builds your profile into a brand that is recognised by prospective customers and industry leaders. It is what you become known for. It sets the context in which prospects and the media engage with you. Your clear positioning and strong market message allow you to charge a premium for your products and services.

In essence, it's marketing made easy.

The 3X Customer Formula

This formula is designed to classify the key factors that allow you to clearly identify who you can sell your products and services to. We begin by identifying the top challenges that they experience in relation to your area of expertise. We then identify the 'outcomes' they would like to achieve and, finally, how best to define them.

This research will allow you to reduce your advertising and marketing costs to a minimum while maximising your profit margins. Begin now by completing the questions posed in table 3.2. Be as specific and focused as you can in narrowing down who your customers are and what they need.

Table 3.2: the 3X Customer Formula template

1 What are the top five challenges your ideal customer experiences in relation to your area of expertise? (e.g. overweight, career slump, lacklustre sales, troubled children, relationship on the rocks)	1 2 3 4 5
2 What are the top five 'outcomes' they would expect from an expert within your field? (e.g. lose 20 kg, get a promotion, boost sales, connect with kids, repair relationship)	1 2 3 4 5
3 How would you define your prospective clients?	Male _____ % Female _____% My area of expertise specifically benefits: • general consumers • small business owners • government • corporations • not-for-profits What area do their challenges fit in? • business • career • love • life What is the subcategory within this area that best describes who they are and what interests them? (e.g. business—social media marketing; career—writing powerful résumés; love—finding the love of your life; life—feeling fit and fabulous) Subcategory: _____ What is the age range for your ideal customers? Between _____ and _____.

(continued)

51

Table 3.2: the 3X Customer Formula template *(cont'd)*

3 How would you define your prospective clients? (*cont'd*)	What is important to them? (e.g. timely service, high quality, personality, an experience, time saving, life transformation, making money). List just three. 1 2 3
	What types of magazines, blogs, newsletters, journals, social media sites or events do they follow, engage with or attend? 1 2 3 4 5 6 7 8 9 10

How does this research translate into bankable products and/or services? By identifying the mindsets of your prospects when they buy, where best to advertise and who to contact for potential exposure — simply put, how to reach your ideal customer cost effectively and with minimum effort.

This research can be used not only to generate sales from online products, but to target companies and conferences to secure paid speaking engagements, which could earn you $2000 to $10 000-plus per engagement, depending on your topic and personal brand. You'll aim to identify media that could potentially feature you in a story that reaches out to hundreds of thousands of prospective customers, and to discover email lists and advertising opportunities that yield high conversion rates, not to mention hosting paid webinars, events or workshops or even getting paid as a top-level consultant.

It all depends on how you would like to create your ultimate lifestyle business and how far you would like to take it.

Sleep for sale—how to buy it by the bucketload

As I walked through Times Square on my way to the media conference, I thought to myself how nice it would be to take off and travel wherever I wanted to and not be limited by lack of funds. What I didn't realise was that I'd just set that process in motion.

Tips and resources

→ Use the ascension marketing model to create a seamless customer experience and a loyal fan base, thereby dramatically increasing your revenue, reach — and free time.

→ To conduct a successful online business, you must get your head around the metrics.

→ To maximise profits you need to understand the mindsets of your prospective clients; using the 3X Customer Formula will help you to define them, the challenges they experience and the outcomes they seek.

For tools, tricks and secrets to creating your very first product, visit www.benangel.com.au/flee9-5 to secure your exclusive 'Get Started' resource guide.

4 RESEARCH
The new world economy — addicted to content

→ Plan, package, produce

There is a simple way to package information that, under the right circumstances, can make it irresistible. All you have to do is find it.
— Malcolm Gladwell

You are now a publisher, just like *Time* magazine, *Vogue* and *The Huffington Post*! And like any publisher, you must find the key to unlocking the greatest challenge facing media companies today—how to make great profits in the new world economy.

In June 2013 Facebook was reported to have 1.15 billion monthly active users. Millions of people are jumping online every single day to post their thoughts about everything from the latest fashion, what they ate and who they hung out with to their political views or sharing how-to tips and lifestyle advice—all of which express who they are as individuals and contribute to their feeling connected, accepted and even revered by friends, family and co-workers. The need for humans to assert their social status (a primal instinct) is shaping the content of our new world economy.

Content is king

Content may be king, but until it's packaged it remains intangible. How much is a piece of advice really worth if you can't physically grasp it? So much depends on how that advice is packaged and marketed. Of course it also depends on the outcome that piece of advice aims to help you achieve. How much would you pay someone to learn how to make a billion dollars? Five thousand dollars, a hundred thousand, a million? The higher the perceived value, the more money some people will be prepared to pay. It's a simple equation.

If you are an agent of influence, content is the key to creating the business—and life—you love. It's what shapes opinions, transforms lives, drives sales and generates mass media. It allows you to flee 9 to 5, because once you have created it you can leverage it in varying formats again and again. An article can become an audio program, a blog can become a book, and a book can become an online course. With each adaptation a new means of leverage presents itself.

Whether you sell products or services, you must now have content for online distribution sites such as Facebook, YouTube, LinkedIn and Twitter, plus your own email communications, media and blogs.

The challenge is to create content that compels people to buy and encourages them to share your message with the world.

Many might view this as an overwhelming task, but I'm here to tell you it's not. With the right systems, processes and support, creating new content that you can package into marketable materials can be fun, and the great news is you can do this work anywhere. I'm sitting on Waiheke Island in New Zealand overlooking a stunning bay while I write this chapter. I don't share this with you to brag (okay, maybe just a little!), but because it exemplifies the Flee 9 to 5 message and lifestyle. Sitting on a beach in the sun, I'm also doing work I love, an activity from which I derive my income.

Having been a writer for more than ten years, I have developed various processes to create content and products. I'll simplify them for you here by introducing you to my content creation system, a series of processes that will make the work feel like a walk in the park instead of a crowbar to the knee. And it will set up you and your brand to receive online sales in no time.

So far in this book we have identified your expertise and knowledge and started to work on your ideas. It's now time to learn how to develop these ideas and package them into marketable products.

Finding the algorithms that deliver: the crucial step almost everyone ignores

In his fascinating book, *Trust Me, I'm Lying: Confessions from a Media Manipulator*, Ryan Holiday explains how there are people in the media who study algorithms to discover the precise headlines and content that will keep your eyeballs glued to their websites. In essence, eyeballs = cash.

So media specialists research the trending topics to find out where the money is and shape content that keeps people stuck in a loop: reading one article, they are enticed by another, and another. People find themselves caught in these infinite loops on Facebook, Twitter, YouTube and other social media sites, and increasingly linked to one another in a complex network that often appears to the user like a single vast source. Content creators understand human behaviour and language, and how to capture and seduce their audience.

We're all addicted to content.

Finding the algorithms that shape our own niche, what's trending and which topics are 'paying' isn't as hard as many believe. Creating addictive content that can shape the world is a formulated process. You simply need to add real heart and soul to the mix to create an authentic experience that shapes how people behave, think and feel.

The answers are right in front of 'you. A simple search on online news sites for your niche will uncover the trending topics. For example, if your area of expertise is business, visit sites such as www.forbes.com and do a search of its trending articles. This will give you an indication of which headlines people are clicking on and furiously liking and sharing. This process allows you to catch and ride the currents, which are made up of a mass of online content that constantly ebbs and flows.

This provides you with the tools and the information to package and produce your content into marketable products. How? By identifying the headlines and the sub-topics in your niche that people want to learn more about. This research not only shapes your products, it shapes how you will market them. It also helps to identify *keywords* to use to find this content online. These are the terms and phrases your audience types into Google on a daily basis to find how-to answers to their problems — problems you will soon be solving with your products, if you're not already.

Going niche, then going broad

Nobody puts Baby in a corner! But what if I told you the corner is where the cash is?

We've all heard someone described as 'a jack of all trades but master of none'. Many experts, in getting started, want to exploit all of their expertise at once. The challenge here is that it makes marketing massively costly, because they are using a 'scatter-gun' approach, firing off round after round in the hope that some will hit the target. But ammunition (marketing) is expensive. Secondly, the media won't touch you: they don't know which box to fit you in because your identity embraces an amalgam of skills. Putting forward just one skill at a time will yield you much better results.

With this in mind, I recommend the following process:

1. Identify your 'overarching' marketing message

What is it that you stand for? (My slogan is 'Shape the world we live in'.) This can be applied to business, career, life and love. Think of a slogan that can ground *all* the work you do, and the expertise and knowledge you possess. Brainstorm 20 ideas, then bring that down to five, then three, then finally one.

2. Identify the tool or strategy you use to deliver your marketing message or generate your outcome

For example, if I was to pick a specific genre, such as business, and focus on my subcategory, publicity, the tool I would use to help people win publicity is *influence*. This tool can be used in various areas, but in this particular case I would teach individuals how it can generate major publicity for their brand and business quickly to help them shape the world we live in. To make it seamless, it should always tie back in with the overarching message of the business.

3. Get known for your main message and *one tool only* within a defined period of time

Give it, say, three to six months before you move on to another genre covered by your *overarching* message. For example, I would spend three months educating my email subscribers and social media channel on influence and how it can be applied to generate publicity. After a set period of time, after becoming known in relation to this particular subcategory, I would switch focus to how to become a paid speaker and the tools required to achieve this, then stick with this subject for a defined period of time before moving on again.

Attacking all subcategories at once confuses your target market. They don't know who you are, what you stand for or, most importantly, why *you* are an agent of influence within your particular genre. Work in waves and each wave will yield you a massive return on investment, particularly when it comes to launching your product.

Think now, what is the genre you're focusing on for one particular product, and which 'tool' are you going to teach people how to use to get results?

Plan, package, produce: winning the trifecta

In horse racing terminology a trifecta is a bet in which the gambler must successfully predict which horses will finish first, second and third, in correct order. If there is a trifecta in content marketing, it is:

1 planning

2 packaging

3 producing.

This is the sequence to follow in order to achieve rapid results. Let's kick off our race with planning.

Planning your way to profits: the vital first step

> *Amateurs sit and wait for inspiration, the rest of us just get up and go to work.*
> — **Stephen King**

Whether you are creating content or a product, the same process applies. This process can be applied to a range of content formats, including blog posts, feature articles, digital products, audio scripts, online courses, keynote presentations and even books. No matter what you are creating, there is always a beginning, a middle and an end.

The Matrix Strategy of Content Creation

I'd spent days listening to Anthony Robbins, trying to work out how he mesmerises his audiences. That man has a tongue that can always seduce. Suddenly I realised what he does. He speaks in a very particular pattern, and it is this pattern that forms the foundation for *all* of the content that has attracted millions of dollars and won him fans around the world. I broke it down into four easy steps and then tried it out for the first time on stage in front of an audience of over 200 in Melbourne, Australia.

They were captivated. They were leaning forward, hanging on every word I said.

Later I wove it into my products — and noticed how much more compelling they had suddenly become. Over the years, I've evolved this to make the planning process and the content even more enjoyable and easy to create.

Let's take a look at how these four steps work.

1 *What and who?* First the content must be introduced. What is it you are going to talk about and what problem do you intend to solve? Pick one product you would like to create and then, in table 4.2 (see p. 65), explain in one sentence *what* you plan on sharing with your audience. For example, 'I will share with you powerful strategies to attract new clients in 30 days or less'. Then introduce *who* you are.

2 *Why?* Now identify *why* you plan on sharing this information with them. For example, it will help them turn their business around and generate new profits within a month.

3 *How?* Next, outline the *how* behind achieving this result — for example, seven steps that help attract new

clients. Outline the specific steps and provide examples of how this information has been or can be applied to your existing clients. If you're just starting out, use industry examples or statistics to provide credibility. Also, weave in stories throughout your product presentation. Share your personal experiences to create connection with your audience at a deeper level.

4 *Why and where to next?* First, explain *why* you shared the *how* information. This contextualises your message and turns your knowledge into a 'packaged' product. Secondly, segue to the next product or service in your ascension marketing model by sharing with them your *where to next* for further information.

Table 4.1 shows an example of how it works.

Table 4.1: the Matrix Strategy of Content Creation (*example*)

Step 1: What and who?	Step 2: Why?
I am Sally Trevase and I am a leader in the field of career development. Today I will share with you … ▪ seven steps to building confidence to help advance your career. Is it okay if I share with you a little about my background and why you should be listening closely …	The reason I will share with you x, y and z is … ▪ in a competitive work environment it is critical that you stand out from your competition so you are first in line for a promotion or pay rise.
Step 3: How?	**Step 4: Why and where to next?**
There are seven steps that must be taken to achieve this, including: **1 develop a powerful personal brand** ▪ Explain how ▪ Provide example ▪ Share story **2 influence outcomes** ▪ Explain how ▪ Provide example ▪ Share story …	The reason I'm sharing these seven steps with you is … ▪ they offer the fastest way to get a promotion and get noticed within your field of work, to get a pay rise, and to gain the attention of key influencers and secure your future. **Follow with segue:** And of course, to learn more about x, y and z, visit [website], buy [product] or speak with me.

This powerful process achieves a number of objectives:

- It makes a potentially overwhelming task manageable and easy.

- It engages the audience by continually reinforcing *why* they need to pay attention to the content, no matter what format it is presented in.

- The case studies, examples, statistics and stories add colour, depth and life to your product or presentation, painting a picture of what's possible when your how-to strategies are applied.

- Depending on how much information you provide in the *how* section, you have just created a seamless upsell to the next product or service in your ascension marketing model, by using real-life examples and case studies as supporting evidence.

You can use this format to write articles, books, audio presentations, keynotes and more. Its potential is limitless. It literally takes your how-to advice and packages it into a marketable product.

And the best thing about this is that it takes only 30 minutes or less to plan a complete product. It automatically simplifies what you are trying to say and condenses it into clear and digestible messages for your audience. Secondly, it infuses your content with credibility by declaring, 'Here is the technique and here's how it can be practically applied'.

Now it's your turn. Pick one of the products you would like to create and complete the template in table 4.2.

Table 4.2: the Matrix Strategy of Content Creation (*your turn*)

Step 1: What and who?		Step 2: Why?
I am _____ and I am a leader in the field of _____. Today I will share with you … Is it okay if I share with you a little about my background and why you should be listening closely …		The reason I will share with you, x, y and z is …
Step 3: How?		**Step 4: Why and where to next?**
There are _____ steps that must be taken to achieve this, including:		The reason I share with you the _____ steps/principles is …
Step 1: _____ ▪ Explain how: ▪ Provide example: ▪ Tell story:		
Step 2: _____ ▪ Explain how: ▪ Provide example: ▪ Tell story:		**Follow with segue:** And of course, to learn more about x, y and z, visit [website], buy [product] or speak with me.
Step 3: _____ (Repeat process for as many steps as you have; 10 steps would represent 10 chapters in a book, then you would repeat the process within each chapter.)		

Packaging: making the 'intangible' tangible

Several years ago a colleague of mine, Rhondalynn Korolak, approached me to help her come up with a title for her upcoming release on accounting and finance.

You can imagine my expression. My first question was, how do we make a topic that sounds so dry and dull into something brand-new and exciting? And that's when it hit me. Let's call it 'Financial Foreplay: Whip Your Business into Shape'. I came up with the cover concept of a leather boot with a whip wrapped around it at the base, with yellow as the background colour. It was an instant bestseller.

It starts with the name

How you package your knowledge and expertise is *everything*. And now you are clearer about the direction your products and information can take, it will be easier to envision how they can be packaged. We start this process by coming up with a compelling name. Once again, you can apply this process to any content, be it an article, book, audio program, workshop, event or digital product. To begin the process use this checklist as your guide.

How to come up with a best-selling product name

- ☐ Research a list of the top 20 best-selling books within your niche, and identify patterns that they have used in the titles (for example, are they outcome based?).

- ☐ Brainstorm 20 product name ideas of your own, using your list for inspiration.

- ☐ Narrow it down to three, then select your number one choice.

- ☐ Create a subtitle that clearly explains the 'outcome' the product aims to achieve (for example, 'Fat Obliterator — How to Lose 7 kg in 7 Days').

- ☐ Write a summary of what the customer will gain by purchasing it.

- ☐ Keep it simple and clear, and focus on the problem your product solves.

Keep it simple, and make it clear what it offers (for example, *Flee 9 to 5, Get Paid 6 to 7 Figures and Do What You Love*. Anyone one chromosome away from a tomato can work out what this book is about. Ensure yours follows suit.

Seduce them with visuals

Once you have a name and a blurb, it's time to package it up by getting your visuals completed. If you're creating a book, you'll need a cover plus an online landing page. This is a web page dedicated purely to promoting this one product, and ideally it will include a promotional video. If you're creating an audio program, you will need a landing page that features a 3D image of the product. Visit www.benangel.com.au/flee9-5 to view active and regularly updated examples of landing pages that have worked.

Branding and packaging are indispensable because their design directly expresses and reflects the quality of your product. Don't cheap out and get your cousin's girlfriend to do the graphics. It could severely decrease your conversion rates and impact your sales.

To help you get your graphic design completed at an affordable rate, I've teamed up with 99designs, a design marketplace where you submit a brief for what you require, then designers from all over the world compete for your work. In many cases you can receive 20 or more proposals for the work you need designed. You then make your choice and the funds are released to the designer. As the buyer you're completely protected. For details on an exclusive offer, visit www.benangel.com.au/flee9-5.

When it comes to design, draw on inspiration from industry experts outside your field. How did they package their products and services? Getting external inspiration often throws up a new twist and breathes new life into an old subject, making you the go-to person in your field.

Producing: first create your production schedule

Whenever you are asked if you can do a job, tell 'em, 'Certainly I can!'
Then get busy and find out how to do it.
— **Theodore Roosevelt**

If you want to get something done, make a public announcement and have your social media networks keep you accountable. In writing my second book, *CLICK — The New Science of Influence*, I decided to announce publicly that I would write that 60 000-word book within 30 days and launch it on my thirtieth birthday, March 30. With the external pressure of others watching my every move and seeking updates on my progress, I found a support network and a valid reason to get it done on time — to avoid public humiliation! Announce your intention publicly, then ask for support. This is about stripping away potential excuses so you can just do it.

Create a production schedule that blocks out set times each day for you to focus on your work. If you're currently working 9 to 5, start by doing just an hour a day in the morning before work or in the afternoon when you have some quiet time to yourself. Make a commitment right now that you will never use time as an excuse to not get it done. This process is about buying back time, and to achieve this an investment is required in the early days. But because you'll be focusing on something you love, it will feel fulfilling to be doing something for yourself.

Create an action list of what's required now to produce your product. By this stage you will have various ideas that you can work on. Revisit your ascension marketing model and begin with your introductory offer, keeping in mind what the next product in line is to seed by way of the segue.

The 60-Minute Expert: using fear as your fuel

People wonder why first-time directors can make a brilliant picture, then suck on the second one. It's because they're a little terrified the first time. So they listen to all the experts around them.
— **James Caan**

Last year I received an email from *GQ* men's magazine requesting my opinion on the career choices of actor Ryan Gosling for an upcoming feature. It had been years since I'd seen a Gosling film (and I couldn't even remember what it was). I was given 60 minutes to prepare for the interview.

With my heart racing I jumped on YouTube and watched the 60-second previews for each of his movies. I could see immediately why he took such roles to develop his personal brand, and how this had impacted his career.

An hour later I conducted the interview, then went about my day as usual. Later that afternoon I received an email of thanks, saying, 'Great work. Rarely is an interview subject as prepared. Appreciate the effort'.

How confident are you in your skills?

To make money you must be credible.

People must take you seriously, but being taken seriously is as much about perception as it is about skillset and content. Combine skills with credibility and you create an authentic, unstoppable brand that drives sales and exposure at little cost. Experts know this and leverage its power.

Positioning individuals to appear in the media as experts is my specialty. The great news is, you can learn on the job. You don't need to know everything there is to know about your topic right now; you just need to know more than your customer or the person interviewing you.

It may take no more than a quick internet search, a telephone call to a colleague or an email to get the answers to your questions. Whether or not you require qualifications within your industry depends on several factors. There are many useful questions you can ask to handle this, including:

- Are there industry standards that you must adhere to, and if so, what is the industry body you should contact to find out more?

- How are you creating your content? Is it from experience, through repurposing of publicly available information, based on your unique story or through interviewing other experts with qualifications within your field? All of these options add credibility to the mix.

- Where is your content sourced? Can you license it or pay an expert to contribute to your material?

- Do you have client case studies and statistics that you can weave into your content to give it credibility and further position you as an expert?

And, most importantly, do you believe in the message, story and strategies that you are delivering?

Only twice in my ten-year career as a professional speaker have I been asked what my qualifications are and if I went to university. Why? Because I believe in what I'm doing and I back it up with evidence and real-world experience that anyone can use to make a real change in their life. Mark Twain put it eloquently: 'I've never let my schooling interfere with my education.'

Education can be bought; experience must be earned.

Set your own curriculum

I feel strongly that continuing education is key to a successful business. I do what I do because I love it, and because I love it I continually educate myself by staying on top of industry trends and searching for new and innovative ways to help my clients. Here are others ways to become an expert:

- Spend 30 minutes each day reading the top industry blogs related to your niche. This information is often more up to date than books, as there can be a massive lag time between a book being written and it being released and read.

- Follow the top experts in your field and find recommended resources or reading to uncover further information on their secret-sauce formulas.

- Write a weekly article using the format outlined in the Matrix Strategy of Content Creation (see p. 62). You'll quickly realise that you already know more than you thought and uncover gaps in your knowledge that you need to fill.

The winning edge

Self-discipline gives you the winning edge when it comes to planning, packaging and producing products and online content that converts. The more you do it, the easier it gets and the more you will enjoy it. Get started now by setting yourself 30 minutes to map out your first 'introductory' product.

Having completed the exercises in each chapter, you'll find this will come together quickly, and with this swift progress you'll suddenly feel that it is all within reach. Keep your end goal in mind each and every day.

Now you know how to monetise your message, it's time to discover how to market it using my 3D Marketing System.

Tips and resources

→ Aim to create content that compels people to buy and encourages them to share your message with the world.

→ Find the headlines and topics that people in your niche want to learn more about, and draw them into infinite loops of engagement.

→ When marketing content, go for the trifecta: plan (using the Matrix Strategy of Content Creation), package (devise an inspired way to 'make intangibles tangible') and produce (draw up and adopt a production schedule and action list).

For up-to-date information, checklists, tools and links to help you create your product, visit www.benangel.com.au/flee9-5.

---

5 MARKET IT
Marketing your message

→ How to build a following of over 35 000

> *Man's mind, once stretched by a new idea,*
> *never regains its original dimensions.*
> — Oliver Wendell Holmes

In 2008 AuthorHouse, a US self-publishing company, signed up more than 40 000 authors, distributed over 60 000 books and sold 2.5 million copies. This sounds like a lot, but it represents an average of only around 42 sales per title.

Today there is a common misconception that a message will market itself if it's captivating enough. That's uncertain at best. An insider contact revealed to me that Rhonda Byrne, the author of the famous bestseller (and movie) *The Secret*, refused to do interviews for media outlets with an audience below one million. She has sold a staggering 19 million copies worldwide, which clearly demonstrates that it's not how much marketing you do that creates success: the key factor is where you focus your efforts. Even His Holiness the Dalai Lama has a publicist to help spread the word about his upcoming book releases and tours.

The public perception is that these successful individuals took their products to market and instantly became best-selling authors without a marketing or PR strategy behind them. But all marketing is not created equal. It's time for us to pull back the curtain to see what it really takes to be successful.

The goal of marketing is not just to focus on the 20 per cent of activities that produce 80 per cent of the results. It's to focus on the 1 to 2 per cent of activities that generate the 98 to 99 per cent of income.

You've got life-changing ideas in your grasp, and now that you're clear on what your message is, and you've discovered how to package it, it's time to monetise it by marketing it like a pro. Think of it as a boulder sitting atop a hill — we need to give it a push to create momentum to get it rolling. I'm going to give you a running start now by providing you with strategies to help you build an online following of 35 000 plus.

To achieve this you need to follow a process in which you first test the viability of your product. Based on the results, you then launch it into a wider market. Finally you put it on autopilot so you can make money while you sleep. Let's begin with…

Phase 1: Test your product—the 7-Day Quick Fire Test

The 7-Day Quick Fire Test allows you to launch a new product on a shoestring budget and assess its potential for generating profits before it is released to a wider market. Testing digital products is quick and painless. There's none of the hassle of testing physical products and delivering them to a shopfront or pop-up store. This initial phase is the most critical as it establishes the foundation for generating six- to seven-figure revenues.

We'll begin by testing your product idea using Facebook, a social media platform that is comprehensively embedded in our society. As an initial text case you can set a budget as low as $25 per day for seven days ($175 total spend). It would be unwise to share with you Facebook's marketing particulars in these pages, given the speed at which its practices change. To learn more about Facebook advertising, and for up-to-the-minute recommended training programs and resources that make it easy even for the novice, visit www.benangel.com.au/flee9-5.

The 7-Day Quick Fire Test campaign aims to ascertain:

- the product's viability and profitability
- the conversion rate
- the success of targeted demographic
- changes to be made to the sales page
- which ads are clicked on most and which copy appeals to the consumer (so that it can be rolled out on a larger scale).

The test is designed to reduce time wastage and speed up the process of taking a product to market (before doing a major launch), which could yield you $20 000 or more within a month. Let's go through it step by step:

1. Pick a platform to market through and a product to promote

Visit www.facebook.com/advertising and create an account for your initial test campaign. (If you are convinced that your target market isn't on Facebook, set up a Google AdWords account by visiting www.google.com/adwords. It takes only a few minutes.) Select a product under the $100 price point. It is critical to choose a product that has a low barrier to entry. Once a customer purchases one of your introductory offers, and rapport and trust have been established, you can then introduce them to your other, more expensive products.

2. Create your ads

Create 10 ad variations to promote your product, and direct the traffic straight to your online sales page. For details on how to set up an online sales page and shopping cart, and to view live examples, visit www.benangel.com.au/flee9-5.

3. Set your budget

Set a budget for how much you would like to spend each day and how much you are willing to pay per click to your web page. Target your 'ideal' customer based on the 3X Customer Formula (see p. 50). If using Google AdWords, visit www. googlekeywordtool.com to find out more about Google's handy tool for finding keywords and phrases that your customers are typing in when searching (such as *how to get new clients, how to find a relationship* or *what to say on a first date*). The more specific you are, the higher your conversion rates will be.

Ensure your keywords and phrases reflect the copy on your sales landing page — an insider tip Google advertising pros rarely share. For Facebook, select your age group and the 'interests' your customers are attracted to (such as *weight loss*, *personal development* or *small business*). Be specific. If this is all new to you, visit www.benangel.com.au/flee9-5 for more information on the ins and outs of getting your campaign set up.

4. Revise and relaunch

Track your ads over a seven-day period and systematically create new ones and shut down ones that aren't being clicked on and aren't yielding sales. Re-create the ads that *are* working and relaunch them by changing one element at a time — that is, first the imagery, then the copy and then the demographic they are marketed to. Finally, and most importantly, use the information from your test to tweak your online sales page. If it completely missed the mark, duplicate this page and create versions a, b, c and d — as many as necessary. As with your ads, change only one thing at a time — for example, the main headline on your sales page; in the next version you could change the sales video script. This isolates and allows you to identify elements that aren't working. Conduct the Quick Fire Test and assess your results a second, third, fourth and fifth time.

Remember, the fastest way to profits is to fail fast, fail early and fail often. Test and measure as you move through this process and continue to tweak, revise and relaunch until you've nailed the winning formula for your specific offering in your specific industry.

To help make things even easier, table 5.1 (overleaf) illustrates a seven-day schedule for your first Quick Fire Test campaign. As you'll soon see, it takes just an hour or less a day over a seven-day period to trial your first product.

Table 5.1: the 7-Day Quick Fire Test schedule

Sunday	Monday	Tuesday	Wednesday	Thursday	Friday and Saturday
	Create 10 new ads. (60 minutes)	Test and measure your ads. Switch off those that aren't working. Re-create those that are, and test one element at a time. (30 minutes) Promote a special offer (e.g. one day only, until midnight tonight save $$). (60 minutes)	Create 10 new ads. (60 minutes)	Test and measure your ads. Switch off those that aren't working. Re-create those that are, and test one element at a time. (30 minutes)	Report on results for week: total sales, profit, conversion rates and average visitor value.

349% ROI on Facebook advertising

In 2013 I launched my 30-Day Business Turnaround Program, designed to provide business owners who were struggling to get new clients with quick and easy marketing strategies that they could implement within an hour or less to help boost their revenue. I conducted an initial test using Facebook advertising. Over a four-week period I invested a total of $1992.26, which generated $6597 in sales — an admirable 349 per cent return on advertising investment. I used the 7-Day Quick Fire Test method and scaled it up over a longer period of time to see if conversion rates would hold. They did.

Creating ads that convert

You may or may not choose to test your product's viability via Facebook or Google AdWords. Either way, you have a finite amount of space in which you can run copy that converts.

Simplifying your marketing message is at the heart of its success. This is where your outcome-focused marketing efforts come full circle. Condense your copy down to its essence as we did earlier (for example, 'how to lose 7 kg in 7 days').

As an illustration, table 5.2 offers an example for each of the four key profit categories discussed earlier — business, career, love and life. Drill down to your subcategories to define them further, and ensure you focus on your customers' outcomes first and foremost.

Table 5.2: examples of ad campaigns that convert

Ad #1: Business	Ad #2: Career
Need leads fast?	Want a promotion?
New system boosts sales by 33%. Click here to see how.	She was promoted within 3 months and got a 19.5% pay rise. Learn how.
Ad #3: Love	Ad #4: Life
Single?	Trim inches off your waist.
This audio helped her put a ring on it. Here's what you need to know.	New plan shows you how to lose 7 kg in 7 days. Learn how here.

Tracking conversions

Now your ad is set up, it's time to put it to the test. But before you do, it's essential that you leverage the tools that Facebook and Google provide you, including conversion tracking. Google and Facebook offer you unique codes that can be embedded on the 'confirmation' page that delivers your product to the customer. This code can then track back to the precise ad that the customer acted on, giving you the power to shut down ads that are getting clicks but no conversions, thereby quickly lowering your costs and increasing your profit margins. A quick online search will provide you or your developer with instructions on how to embed this code on your site from the relevant advertising platforms. In most cases it's as simple as copying and pasting a line of code.

For a list of insider tips, tools and resources to make the most out of your 7-Day Quick Fire Test campaign, visit www .benangel.com.au/flee9-5.

Critical mass marketing: the tsunami effect

> *When an idea reaches critical mass there is no stopping the shift its presence will induce.*
> — **Marianne Williamson**

Most entrepreneurs proactively seek the elusive tipping point at which a new idea or product finds its own momentum and hits critical mass. Now you understand the simple process of developing an idea, packaging it and then testing it in the marketplace, it's time to uncover strategies that create a tsunami-like effect when launching it.

A well-tested product should be taken to the marketplace at full force.

After all, it has the potential to provide you with your annual salary within a space of a few short weeks or months.

Where many go wrong is in launching their product gradually, so they make ripples in the marketplace that last only momentarily, as if they were skimming stones across a lake's surface. Launching a product for the first time not only establishes you in the market, it potentially creates a tipping point at which other opportunities are born. It provides established agents of influence with the opportunity to reinvent a potentially dying brand. Take Miley Cyrus, for example.

Building the buzz: what we can learn from Miley Cyrus's VMA publicity stunt

Miley Cyrus gave a controversial, sexually provocative performance at the 2013 Video Music Awards in which she violated a large foam finger (and my eyes) live on stage. Was this a young lady heading down the same path of self-destruction Britney Spears took when she shaved off her hair? Hardly. This strategic move made an artist who had almost completely fallen into obscurity the talk of the world.

Miley's second single, 'Wrecking Ball', from her new album, *Bangerz*, was strategically released the very next day and subsequently downloaded more than 90 000 times, breaking records by garnering 19.3 million video views in its first day online. Three weeks and 175 million views later, Miley had successfully re-established herself as an artist to be reckoned with by stealing the limelight from Lady Gaga's new release, *Applause*, and Katy Perry's *Roar*.

Even though her stunt attracted worldwide criticism, Cyrus achieved her objective: her sales went through the roof in spite of serious competition. Personal responses aside, it's impossible to argue that Miley didn't pull off a supremely successful marketing campaign, the likes of which we haven't seen in years. When launching a new product, we can surely learn from it. Above all, Miley's timing was impeccable. Most entrepreneurs fail to recognise that timing can make or break a launch, and good timing can increase a fan base by thousands. You'll learn more about this in phase 2 (overleaf).

As a dear friend, professional speaker Joanna Martin, puts it, when it comes to launching an event, 'There's not one way to put fifty people in a room. There's fifty ways to put one person in a room'. Whatever the format — whether an event, book, online course or digital download — the same principles apply when launching a new product or service. Two types of marketing campaigns that can help are the *enlightened launch* and the *evergreen campaign*.

Phase 2: Launching your product to the wider marketplace: the enlightened launch

An enlightened launch is designed to educate your prospects about your area of expertise using the 'tool' we outlined in earlier steps to help them achieve the desired outcome. It also builds the need for them to learn more, anticipation to purchase when the product becomes available, and the trust and credibility required to gain high conversion rates.

Let's look at an example. Sally is an expert in leadership who helps small business owners effectively manage their teams and drive profits. To launch her principal product, a four-week online leadership course valued at $197, Sally launches a free three-part series on 'leadership to profits'. She creates this free content by using the Matrix Strategy for Content Creation, as outlined in chapter 4. She decides that she will deliver this series via three short educational videos that are approximately eight to ten minutes long—short enough to keep viewers engaged while not giving away all her best content. To launch her product, Sally follows the enlightened launch framework (see figure 5.1).

This framework is popular among the world's biggest agents of influence. Marie Forleo, for example, has a Facebook fan base of over 85 000 and a YouTube subscriber base of 60 000 plus. Her quirky nature and business angle of 'create a business and life you love' have seen her featured alongside Oprah Winfrey on Super Soul Sundays. She made the kind of crossover to television that few achieve, by successfully marketing herself and her products in a way that built mass momentum and traction in the marketplace. Other agents of influence using this framework include Anthony Robbins, Janet Switzer, Brendon Burchard and Armand Morin, along with many major companies that are household names.

The enlightened launch framework generates millions for some of the most successful agents of influence in the business through a strategy that involves seven key ingredients.

Figure 5.1: the enlightened launch framework

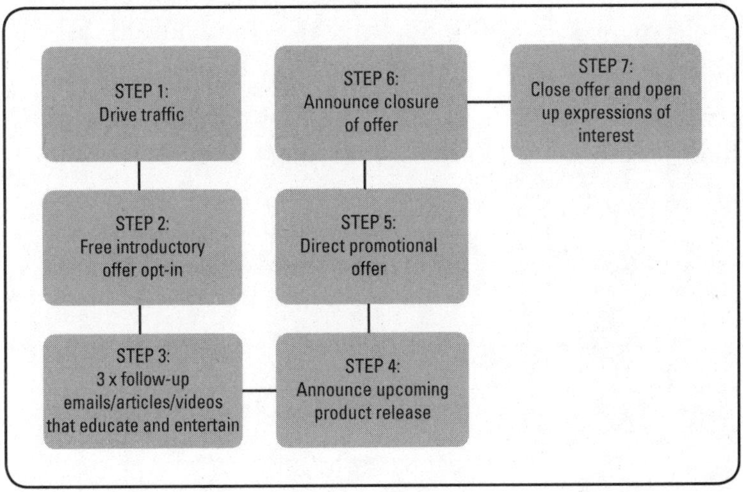

1. Drive traffic

The core goal of any successful product launch is to drive qualified traffic to opt in to your complimentary series. A marketing mix will generate the best outcome. In chapter 3 we discussed the 2.3 per cent litmus test (the industry average for online conversions). Work out now how many visitors you need to your sales page to generate a 2.3 per cent conversion.

For example, Sally wants to generate 300 sales. We first look at how many sales per thousand visitors she can make at this rate (approximately 23). We then divide 300 by 23 (13), and multiply 13 by 1000 for a total of 13 000, which is the number of visitors to her sales page required to generate approximately 300 sales and (based on a unit price of $197) $59 100 in revenue.

After your 7-Day Quick Fire Test campaign, you will have an idea of what conversion rate you can expect for your enlightened launch. In my experience, a launch process such as this can yield conversion rates as high as 4.5 to 18 per cent. However, to help minimise our risk we always calculate a worst-case scenario so we know how much we are willing to spend to generate the required traffic to the sales and opt-in pages.

Use the formula set out in table 5.3 to calculate how much traffic you will need to reach your financial objectives.

Table 5.3: traffic calculation formula

Target unit sales **Unit price**	_____ $_____.____
Test campaign conversion rate	_____%
How many sales per 1000 visitors can you make?	1000 divided by ___% conversion rate = _____
Divide target unit sales by sales per 1000 visitors; multiply by 1000.	Number of website visitors required is _____ Potential revenue from product (target unit sales × unit price) = $_____.____

Now that it's clear how much traffic is required, it's time to look at cost-effective options for driving it to your enlightened campaign. This is where research kicks in. Research the following marketing opportunities and outline the approximate costs for each in an Excel spreadsheet. You can then work back to identify the most affordable options that will generate the return on investment required. If your budget is minuscule, remember that you can negotiate for longer payment terms with some advertisers (such as industry groups and other businesses that deal directly with your target market), or offer commission payouts to affiliates that promote your product. Here are 17 powerful marketing options to get you started:

- Facebook ads
- Facebook-promoted posts
- Twitter posts
- email campaigns to affiliated databases
- email advertising—purchasing ads in industry newsletters
- Google AdWords
- Google Display Network (banner advertising across Google's platform)
- LinkedIn ads
- YouTube sponsored videos
- referral marketing
- re-marketing (this practice involves embedding code on your website; when a prospect visits your site but doesn't purchase, it will target that user on other channels such as Facebook. Visit www.adroll.com to find out more)
- banner advertising purchased on specific blogs
- media buying (for bulk-buying ads online, the preferred sources in the industry are www.sitescout.com, www .buysellads.com and www.adshuffle.com)
- blogging (post regular updates and how-to articles that build the need for your upcoming release. Share links to these posts via social media)
- guest blogging (approach influential bloggers within your sphere who have access to your target market and offer them articles they might like to post)

- sponsored tweets (yes, did you know that you can get major celebrities such as Kim Kardashian to tweet about your product launch? You can visit www .sponsoredtweets.com for details and pricing)

- Outbrain (Outbrain.com is an article marketing site that can serve up links to your articles on major news channel sites. By choosing carefully, you can target highly qualified leads. Visit www.outbrain.com for details).

2. Free introductory offer opt-in

Your complimentary opt-in offer is the critical first experience with your brand. Once people opt in by providing an email address via a 'splash page' (an introductory page on a website that features only one product, service or message) promoting your introductory step, they are automatically entered to receive the scheduled release of free information. I will promote a specific launch date for a series to kick-off and give myself a two- to three-week lead time to attract as many new opt-ins as possible using the strategies outlined in step 1.

3. 3X follow-up

Now you have people subscribing to your free series, it's time to launch it. Release your three-part series over a ten-day period so as not to overwhelm your prospects with too much information, but also not so far apart that the momentum and excitement are lost. Announce in a segue in the second and third parts of your series that you have an upcoming release.

4. Announce upcoming product release

Once your three-part series has run its course, send an email announcing that your product is to be released within

48 hours and that customers will have a limited time to take up your offer, which may include an exclusive launch bonus for the first 300 people who buy. The day before your product release send a second email to your new subscriber list, alerting them that there's only 24 hours to go.

5. Direct promotional offer

It's launch day. Send an email and announce via all social media channels that people can now buy your product. Drive them directly to your sales page. Promote it through as many channels as possible and provide a countdown for how long they have to purchase (for example, 'the first 300' or 'before 5 pm on Friday'). I will generally allow a campaign like this three weeks to run its course and provide myself with as much time as possible to secure sales through as many channels as I can within this period.

6. Announce closure of offer

As the closure of your offer draws near let people know (for example, 'only 37 copies left' or 'only 24 hours to go'). This is where you will generate a second major wave of sales. Don't give up now — it's when the tsunami effect truly kicks in. Dedicate as much time as possible to ensuring *everyone* in your target market knows you've just launched a new product. This campaign could potentially generate you five figures in sales within a three-week period. But don't discount the potential revenue from these individuals going on to purchase your other products over the course of a year. This is your six- to seven-figure business right here.

7. Close offer and open up expressions of interest

Now the offer has closed, instead of sending people to your sales page, send them to a page that says, 'Oops! Too late. Register your expression of interest here to receive details on upcoming releases'. This fills your funnel with prospects for next time.

Enlightened launch FAQs

Won't people get sick of receiving all my emails? Yes, but only those who are not interested buyers.

Do free bonuses with purchase actually work? Absolutely. Products launched without bonuses can generate up to 50 per cent less in sales. Don't risk it. A bonus could be a complimentary audio program, templates, worksheets or even a free webinar. Get creative and make it of high perceived value, and give customers how-to advice or information that they might otherwise have trouble finding.

Should I have a guarantee on my product? Yes. Risk reversal is key in a launch campaign. We want to pull down any barriers to entry and get individuals who wouldn't normally purchase over the line. This could be a seven-day trial, a money-back guarantee or a cancel-anytime offer. It should make you nervous. It also provides the impetus needed for you to make sure that your product is one of the best in the business. Guarantees instantly increase the perceived value of your product, demonstrate credibility and increase conversion rates. The percentage of refunds you will be asked to provide is minuscule. In the past 12 months my refund rate has sat at under 0.025 per cent. Increasing conversion rates by 5 per cent upwards, it is well worth the return on investment.

At this point in the game you may feel slightly overwhelmed. Don't worry.

Clarity always comes after confusion, but more importantly — action.

Allow yourself time to think about what we have covered to date, then strategically map out your next steps as outlined in the following chapters of this book.

Doing an enlightened product launch is not for the faint of heart, and it isn't a short-term strategy. It requires significant attention to detail, energy and focus. Being deliberate and strategic in your approach will ensure your efforts are rewarded.

In phase 1, the 7-Day Quick Fire Test, you trialled your first product before you went to mass market. The enlightened product launch is phase 2 in what is a three-phase process to fleeing 9 to 5 and generating profits on autopilot. Now for the final step.

Phase 3: Put your profits on autopilot: the evergreen anatomy

If launching a product is hard, putting it on autopilot is a walk in the park. Agents of influence depend for their success on creating income while they sleep, which frees up their time to focus on living the life they choose. In phases 1 and 2, you tested your product on a small audience then upscaled to a larger one. Most critically, you now have access to statistics such as conversion rates and which marketing copy and channels have and haven't worked — the holy grail of marketing.

It's now time to extract the 'best of' from phases 1 and 2 and turn them into an automated marketing campaign that has been well tested before launch. This is called the Evergreen Marketing System. This system automates your entire launch process and takes you out of the many processes. It includes:

- establishing ongoing Google AdWords or Facebook ad campaigns that continually, day in and day out, introduce people to your free series, constantly filling your sales funnel

- triggering the product launch whenever people opt in, without any involvement from you, by automating the emails you created during your initial launch campaign using a series of auto-responders. (Visit www.benangel .com.au/flee9-5 for a list of the top email service providers that support an Evergreen Marketing Campaign.)

This three-step process allows you to follow a methodical path designed to create a quick boost to your cash flow, followed by a consistent income stream. And because of your work with the ascension marketing model, each time a customer purchases a product they are upsold to the next, allowing you to continually improve on your profit margins from the original marketing spend. The Evergreen Marketing System, then, fully automates the entire process — all you need do is ensure that people are opting in to your free educational series on a daily basis.

Later, whenever you introduce new products, repeat this three-step process and once and for all take the guesswork out of monetising your knowledge and expertise.

Tips and resources

→ To market like a pro, first assess the viability and potential of your product on a shoestring budget using the 7-Day Quick Fire Test.

→ Next, launch your product to the wider marketplace, using the enlightened launch framework to educate your prospects, build anticipation, and develop trust and credibility.

→ Finally, put your profits on autopilot, automating most of your business processes using the evergreen marketing system to build a consistent income stream and free up your time to pursue your chosen lifestyle.

Visit www.benangel.com.au for further resources relating to this chapter.

6 AUTOMATION
The agent's lifestyle

→ Travel and work from anywhere in the world

To enjoy life, you don't need fancy nonsense, but you do
need to control your time and realize that most things just
aren't as serious as you make them out to be.
— **Timothy Ferriss**, *The 4-Hour Workweek*

The news had just broken. Hurricane Sandy was predicted to arrive within the week. The publicity summit had finished the day before the news alert. I was exhausted. Thankfully my friend Alex had just arrived in New York from Melbourne, and I made the decision to relocate and stay with him in Greenwich Village. For a break, we made our way to 46th Street to visit Schmackary's for some 'lip-schmackin' good' cookies. Biting into a Sch'mores (honey graham base, semisweet chocolate, toasted marshmallow) was better than sex. The melted marshmallow on top gave me respite from the week that was. For ten minutes I ate my emotions, savouring every second.

On top of the impending storm that was making its way towards Manhattan, another one was brewing back home. I had the impression my business partner had completely checked out and none of the marketing was getting done, other than that email I'd sent at 2 in the morning. I was now controlling it all from NYC. My gut told me that the partnership was about to hit the skids. I'd had enough. It was time to put in place measures to stabilise the business, while Alex and I focused on our own safety and our rapidly changing travel arrangements ... because New York was about to shut down!

Mayor Bloomberg announced that the power could be out for over a week and communications could also be affected. The picture of the Statue of Liberty hiding behind her concrete base going viral didn't ease my concerns.

I contacted my virtual assistant and outlined to him what needed to happen for when I went off the grid indefinitely.

I summarised customer service steps and provided all the information he needed to successfully answer queries without my assistance.

Then I took myself out of the picture. With my business partner out of the picture, I was forced to maximise my productivity and let go of control. Outsourcing was the key and the only option. It established systems and processes that I still use today, greatly increasing my freedom to do what I want, knowing that things will be taken care of if I fall sick, am in transit, need time off or get stuck in another hurricane! The moral?

Don't wait for a hurricane to hit before you decide to outsource.

Like everything I share with you in this book, you implement it once and leverage it forever. Welcome to the world of automated economics and outsourcing. Off to India we go.

Automated economics: the art of going off the grid

Mae West once said, 'You only live once, but if you do it right, once is enough'. In 2005 my father, Steele Angel, was diagnosed with a brain tumor. He passed away four short and traumatic weeks later, at the age of 52. He lived more than most in his short time on Earth. His death inspired me to reassess *everything* — how I spent my time, who I spent it with, and why. There's so much in life to experience, see and do — I just had to find a way to do it.

With all the online tools and systems and information in the world at our fingertips, there is no need to live a life devoid of life. We get one shot. Take it, with pure focus and prudent planning. Automated economics (AE) is the process by which we streamline, leverage and automate as many moving parts in a business as possible, with the objective of generating revenue without our constant input. We can then take ourselves off the grid and still make money and continue to grow our businesses.

In our journey together, we have removed the clutter around your goals, knowledge and expertise so we can market the essence of what you do and how you do it. It's now time to strip back the business model to its core functions so others can run it without having to reinvent the wheel each time a new customer query hits your inbox.

You won't have to experience the frustration and overwhelm many entrepreneurs face, because I'm going to show you my secrets for magnifying, mastering and multiplying your results using the power of outsourcing and automated economics. You'll quickly learn how to achieve more in less time, rid your business of time-consuming and repetitive tasks, and build your profile and profits.

It's time we looked at the anatomy of AE so you can gain more time for living your life. We'll begin by taking a look at the automated economics blueprint (see figure 6.1).

Following on from the product launch formula and evergreen marketing system, the automated economics blueprint has five distinct phases. Of the five phases, three are fully automated using online tools, while two require management and need to be outsourced. These two processes, lead- and traffic-generation and customer support, can provide the greatest headaches if not handled well. Outsourcing these successfully can free up your time and generate more income, allowing you to live the Flee 9 to 5 lifestyle.

Figure 6.1: the automated economics blueprint

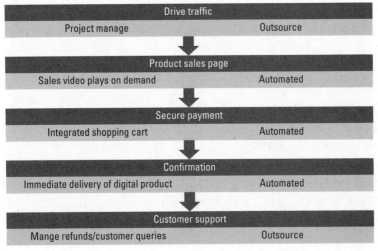

The six steps to automated economics

These six steps will help free your time, your mindset and your life. Becoming the architect of your own domain is about self-mastery in full flight, and here you finally get your wings.

1. Outsource, outsource and outsource

The transition from paid employee to business owner can be more shocking than seeing Joan Rivers in HD. Companies have processes in place to transition employees successfully through their careers. While there is support for new start-ups, there isn't the support needed to make the mindset shift from wage to revenue.

Making money in the online arena works in three phases, each of which involves a shift in mindset and brings its own level of fear and discomfort. Phase 1 is breaking the $1000-per-month in sales mark, phase 2 the $10 000 per month mark, and phase 3 the $20 000 per month milestone. Once you recognise you can earn $10 000 a month from your online products, the momentum takes over; it's then simply a matter of scaling up.

It's critical, however, to keep your emotions in check through each phase. The more money you spend on advertising that has been tested and measured, the more you will earn. Those starting their own business for the first time, who have been used to receiving an average hourly wage of AU$16.37 (or US$7.25), don't necessarily appreciate the need to invest in a website, advertising and education to upskill and upscale, because their employer has covered these bases in the past. The shift from employee to investor/owner will take many a while to get used to. Failing to invest in the right areas, particularly outsourcing key activities, will inhibit progress. The reality is that you can't do it all yourself, but you can project manage it all and outsource cost-effectively, even if you are starting from scratch on a shoestring budget.

You can hire virtual assistant (VA) support staff from services such as Get Friday from as little as $7.50 per month on a monthly payment plan, or hire them as required from $15 an hour (at the time of writing). Your own time is better spent marketing and promoting your products than doing admin that others could be doing for less than it would cost you to do it.

Start outsourcing on a small scale and build it up as your business grows.

With time you will become comfortable with the process and your newfound assistant(s).

2. Plan before hiring virtual assistants

It's important not to rush into outsourcing your work. Before hiring anyone, whether on commission or on a salary, you must know exactly what role you need them to play in your business. Remember that the people you employ will effectively become the face of your business, so decide whether you want them to stay behind the scenes handling the admin work or to deal directly with your clients. They could be:

- project managing marketing campaigns
- dealing with online customer service
- managing admin and bookkeeping.

Each role plays an integral part in maximising profits, customer service, and ongoing product and service sales. While you may have filled each of those roles since the inception of your business, by now you will realise that you can't do it all. Parts of your business are being neglected while you handle the routine work, and as a result your income is dropping. One key aspect to the Flee 9 to 5 lifestyle must be considered — how you're contactable.

A phoneless world

My business partner did end up exiting the business, at which point I decided to downsize everything and use only one virtual assistant. I also made the decision to take the phone number off the website altogether. I live in a phoneless world. I don't have a long list of people to call back. Why? It's no longer necessary. Customers can contact us via email, Twitter, Facebook, YouTube, Instagram and more. Adding telephone to the communication pool didn't speed up the process; it slowed it down.

Even using an answering service is counterproductive. Why get someone to field your calls, only to forward the messages on to you via email anyway? Better that the enquirer email customer support directly so their issue can be resolved then and there, instead of waiting for someone to call them back. Working in different time zones can have an impact too. Phones were a means of communication that I came to see as completely unnecessary for my business, when I could use automated tools and online FAQ pages to resolve issues before they escalated up the chain to me unnecessarily.

Another key element of the traditional business model can be removed in the new economy, saving you a great deal of time.

Welcome to the meetingless world

Meetings are a waste of time unless you are closing a deal. There are so many ways to communicate in real time or asynchronously that any meeting you actually sit for should have a duration and set outcome before you agree to go.
— **Mark Cuban** *(owner of Dallas Mavericks and CEO of HDNet)*

I average one or two face-to-face meetings a month. I used to meet with prospects all the time, until I realised how much time and money it was costing me. A one-hour meeting isn't a profitable way to spend your time. Throw in travel time and it can end up costing you three hours of productive time. In three hours you could write and send an email that brings in $5000 or more. If you do have to meet, however, here are my recommendations:

- *Email.* Could the individual's questions be better outlined within an email with clear action steps? In most cases a follow-up is sent after a meeting. The meeting becomes an unnecessary element in the equation that can automatically be bypassed.

- *Skype*. Can you conduct the meeting over Skype instead? This cuts out travel time and you still get to build rapport and save time. Even Oprah Winfrey used Skype to interview guests live on her show. Eliminating the need to send out camera crews or fly in guests, Skype could save tens of thousands of dollars. Take Oprah's lead and leverage the many online tools you have available to you.

- *Qualify*. Set your boundaries. As your profile begins to build, every man and his dog will want to swing off the coat-tails of your success. If someone requests a meeting, ask them what the objective is. This isn't rude — it's business. If they're not serious, in most cases they simply won't reply. You've just automatically disqualified them and saved yourself a few hours of unproductive time. If they want to do business with you but aren't clear on the details, request a proposal. In 99.9 per cent of cases, I've found, they never get back to you. Only the serious players follow through. Don't be swayed by 'potential' opportunities if they can't outline clearly what they hope to achieve in the first instance.

What are your actions really costing you?

Lachlan, a photographer, spent 80 per cent of his time at business-to-business networking events. On the face of it this sounds like a solid strategy. Not so much when you do the maths. Lachlan's clients were coming straight from referrals outside of these events. Calculating the cost of the event and how much his time was worth per hour, he was throwing away $150 with each one he attended. By attending five or more per week, he was not only wasting time in transit, but losing hundreds of dollars every week and thousands per year. With the business teetering on the edge of bankruptcy, he had to be ruthless in how he spent his time.

(continued)

> ### What are your actions really costing you? (cont'd)
>
> This particular strategy had brought his rate down to less than $10 per hour in total — it would have been more profitable for him to work at McDonald's than to network in a way that failed to produce actual outcomes. By targeting prospects online, his reach would have been more focused and better leveraged, producing greater overall results and buying him back his time.

A false sense of security

Busyness distracts us from what's really important and can create a false sense of security: I'm busy, therefore I'm productive. This is rarely the case and is often more of an avoidance tactic than a business strategy.

Prioritisation of time is key. Only spend your time on activities that will broaden your reach on a large scale, as Rhonda Byrne did in promoting *The Secret*, when she leveraged her time and reach within a defined period of time. Once you have managed these aspects, identify what you can outsource. By doing this you've just significantly increased your profit margin and bought back time.

3. Define expectations

Hiring VAs without setting expectations from the outset is a gamble at best. In selecting a person or a company to take over one or two of your business functions — in this case, primarily customer service and lead generation — you need to have a clear idea of what the job involves, what skills are required and whether the role is suitable for someone other than you to manage. In understanding the tasks yourself, you can lead by example.

Here are the questions to answer before you go on your hiring expedition:

- What experience must they have in this field?
- What specific skills will they need?
- Do they require natural sales ability, or customer service and order-taking experience?
- What hours/days will they be required to work?
- Can they write clearly and grammatically?
- Are they suited to administrative duties?

Make your expectations clear before selecting a VA. If they can't meet them, they're not the right person to begin with. Keep searching.

4. Identify policies and procedures for your lifestyle business

It's not reasonable to expect a new team member to walk in and take over your work without some instruction on what the job entails. For every job, particularly customer service or traffic generation, there are key activities and processes that need to be completed, but many of these are so routine that you do them without thinking.

List your daily tasks and outsource your life — it's time to let go.

List all your daily action tasks for one entire month — every single one of them, including processing payments, reporting and researching advertising options. Leave no stone unturned. Write down exactly what you do and the step-by-step process by which you do it. This will initially be time-consuming, but after one month you will have put together a complete procedures manual for your business that you can then hand over to a qualified team member. You will have freed yourself from routine tasks to focus on other income-producing activities. And as you can outsource the bulk of these tasks for around $10 per hour to virtual assistant providers such as www.getfriday.com/benangel, it hardly makes sense to do them yourself.

Driving traffic

All activities related to driving traffic to your product page can be automated or outsourced. They will need to be project managed by you, however. You are in control and must know and understand where everything is at any time — even if it's simply logging in to check your sales for the day.

These activities include:

- researching lead generation options
- providing recommendations, then implementing them
- reporting on weekly statistics, including sales conversions, advertising spend, what worked, what didn't, and recommend steps forward
- uploading and scheduling social media content
- uploading articles/videos to blog
- approaching other bloggers to secure a guest post
- creating Facebook ads
- keyword research
- tracking and testing adverts.

Customer service

Some 99.9 per cent of customer service enquiries can be responded to via 'canned' and automated responses, which are pre-written to address frequently asked questions, issues and refunds. Document the processes for:

- processing and responding to refunds

- product questions

- customer complaints

- frequently asked questions (making sure you provide them with the knowledge to refer people to blog posts or specific products that answer their queries without intervention from you)

- partnership enquiries

- media enquiries

- troubleshooting customer issues (for example, they can't download product or it won't open in their browser; both issues should have the same solution, which can be posted to an FAQs page).

Empower your VAs with the right information and they'll reward you by giving you more time and helping you make more money in the long and short term.

5. Learn: education = cash flow

Education is at the heart of bringing in six- to seven-figure revenues. The great news is that you don't have to know everything yourself—you just need to manage others who do. For example, say you want to learn about media buying and Facebook advertising. You could, as I have done, purchase online courses (visit www.benangel.com.au/flee9-5 for my recommendations) and get your VA to undertake the training themselves. Then all you need do is get them to summarise what they have learned and you can approve the recommendations they have made.

Furthermore, you can create your own in-house training resources in minutes by using screencast tools such as Screeny for Mac to record your online processes with a voiceover giving directions. Upload using a private YouTube link and give your assistants the link. You can record this at any time, and no matter where your VAs are in the world, they can access it without interrupting you as you work on the bigger ideas that truly make a difference to establishing yourself in the marketplace.

6. Take control: my top six favourite tech tools for agents on the go

According to eMarketer's 2013 estimate on media consumption among US adults, average time spent with digital media per day will soon surpass TV viewing for the first time. With an average of five hours spent online daily, it's easy to waste away a day, a week or even a year in the clutches of the internet. While technology on many levels has destroyed productivity, it can also increase it immensely when you take back control of the beast.

To make your life easier and help you to live the ultimate Flee 9 to 5 lifestyle, here are my top recommended platforms:

- *Hootsuite.* For managing all your social media accounts, Hootsuite.com is my top pick. It can also consolidate the individual messages you receive from all of your accounts, so you can easily reply to them in one hit via the dashboard. With solid reporting tools and access on the go, you'll know at a glance what's working and what isn't.

- *Evernote.* I've mentioned this application several times already in these pages. I can't even begin to express how easy this has made my life. My entire business plan is mapped out using Evernote, and is always accessible and updatable from my Android device on the run. (It's also available for Mac.)

- *Infusionsoft.* You'll need a website, auto-responders and an affiliate program, and ideally you'll manage it from just one location. Infusionsoft is my top recommendation for this. Avoid using too many different online tools for your website, as this can create unnecessary procedures. Consolidation is king.

- *Google Drive.* Losing data can be devastating. After a cup of tea spilt on my laptop and almost derailed my national tour last year, I know this from bitter experience. I back up word documents to the cloud using Google Docs. You can update and manage documents in real time, allowing key players in your projects access as you deem fit.

- *Gmail.* All my customer service queries arrive in our Gmail account, which my VAs can access at any time of the day, including weekends. You can manage your inbox into folders and assign emails to particular individuals for processing, and you can see at a glance who needs replying to and who has already been taken care of.

- *Skype.* The world's most popular internet phone service can be downloaded to your iPhone or Android. It's a fantastic way to keep call costs low when travelling; this is great for the agent on the go.

Draw up your Flee 9 to 5 timeline

The price of anything is the amount of life you exchange for it.
— **Henry David Thoreau**

At this stage in the book you have passed the point of no return. You understand how to buy back your time and your life. It's now time to start working on your timeline, setting out when you're going to take serious action, if you haven't already. Get a yearly wall planner and map out when you are going to create your first product and when you'll launch it.

Begin with the end in mind and leverage outsourcing and digital tools to help produce results faster.

See beyond 9 to 5 and ask yourself the following questions:

- How much money do I need to live on each month?

- How much money do I need as a backup (say, three months' reserve)? (Every business has a 'burn rate': in the early stages it requires greater investment. Prepare for this and avoid taking unnecessary risks.)

- How much will I outsource in the early stages and what will I do myself?

- At what specific point will I flee 9 to 5? (For example, it could be when you begin to make x in monthly sales consistently for a minimum of six months.)

Do the maths, calculate your budget, create your product map and draw up your timeline. It's time to take the leap.

Killed by consulting — a cautionary tale

I used to be lured by the evil that is high-paid consulting work — until I realised it was almost sending me broke and holding back my profit-making. While I love working with high-paying clients, I will work with only one or two at a time. Why? Because at this level it is imperative that a high service standard be met. This in itself can take time away from your other income-producing activities — the returns on which, when fully established, will far outweigh those from consulting.

The other risk faced by many is it takes only one or two clients to drop out to undo a business that relies on them as its primary source of income. Creating digital products is a way to recession-proof your business and stabilise the rollercoaster ride that consulting can sometimes be. I encourage everyone to focus on stabilising their income first, before going for high-risk projects. This is about minimising risk and increasing long-term return on investment.

In every business it is critical to diversify your product or service offerings. Relying on only one creates a 'single point of failure' that could undo all your hard work. By creating a suite of digital products, you always have something to sell and you never need fall into the trap of exchanging time for money.

Tips and resources

→ Through automated economics you can streamline, leverage and automate many moving parts of your business, allowing you to go off-grid while still growing the business.

→ Outsourcing the two main processes that still require management — lead- and traffic-generation and customer support — frees up your time, allowing you to live the Flee 9 to 5 lifestyle.

→ Create your own in-house training resources for your virtual assistants. You don't have to know everything yourself — you just need to manage others who do.

Visit www.benangel.com.au/flee9-5 for my recommendations on online courses on media buying and Facebook advertising.

7 GET SOCIAL
Social media mastery

→ Get primal, get fans, get paid

> *Be less curious about people and more curious about ideas.*
> — **Marie Curie**

Have you ever wondered why it's called a status update or even why social media is so addictive? It's because they appeal to a primal human instinct — to assert our status and establish our position in the social pecking order. Driven by the reptilian brain, our unconscious goals are to procreate and do what's needed to support ourselves and our families, and to continue our genetic line. Our supposedly evolved minds still respond to these primordial instincts. This compels us to share who we are with the world at large through the clothes we wear, the car we drive, the neighborhood we live in, the networks we surround ourselves with, the airline we fly with, the clubs we belong to, the restaurants we frequent, the music we listen to, the movies we watch and the partners we choose to nest with.

In addition to asserting ourselves in the traditional 'tribal' sense in the real world, we've taken to the digital sphere to fulfil this most basic need for status assertion by posting external expressions of who we believe ourselves to be — online for the rest of the world to see. Even if you claim that you don't buy brand-name clothes because you don't believe in labels, you are still asserting your status and beliefs to your digital friends to help determine where you fit in your social network. It's inescapable. We all do it, consciously or not.

Social media is as addictive as crack for our generation. Its omnipresence provides us with a distribution platform to fulfil a basic primal need.

How often have you found yourself obsessed with the number of 'likes' one of your updates has garnered, and the social acceptance it represents? It almost makes you feel sick just thinking about it. Could we really be this vain? Or could it be that we're simply not as evolved as we believe ourselves to be?

Whichever way you look at it, millions upon millions have flocked to these platforms to share their lives online. And, although these media will continue to evolve, our need to express ourselves through them in relation to both our daily lives and our businesses will only become more entrenched. Because of this we will continue to find opportunities to connect and share our messages with an ever-growing audience of like-minded individuals.

SSA—Status Seekers Anonymous

What we must understand in this newly shaped world is that just as you seek to express yourself through the brands, events, people and agents of influence you connect with as an extension of yourself, they too are seeking to express themselves through who *you* are as a brand. Are you akin to Coke or Pepsi, Lady Gaga or Madonna? Are you comparable to industry experts within your niche?

We must be aspirational and appeal to our customers' or clients' primal instincts to help them assert their status through association with us via our products and services and the messages we share to shape the world we live in. In knowing this we unlock the true essence of what social media marketing is—primal instinct on steroids. It is more critical than ever to differentiate ourselves online with a solid 'personality' that helps us to stand out. Social media is as much about personality as it is about psychology—the two are intertwined. And the stronger the message you take to market, the more successful you will be.

The reality-show effect: why revealing 'behind the scenes' will put money in your pocket

Reality shows have taken our TV channels by storm because they appeal to our desire to fit in and feel normal. Revealing 'behind the scenes' information about your journey, the highs and lows (within reason), will garner more attention and in many cases more respect than remaining tight-lipped ever will. Reveal your flaws and watch your fan base support you — you've just connected with them in a way no one else has dared to do for fear of being judged. Don't lash out at others or provide 'sensitive' personal information, but do allow them a peek behind the curtain, at the challenges you face in your life and industry. Many of you may have seen photos of me battling tiredness in juggling writing this book and filming for two TV shows. These types of posts always get a higher engagement level than those that are simply positive, because people can relate to struggle.

Social media has provided us not only with a way in which we can express ourselves, but with an expanding tool to grow our businesses, secure media coverage, attract high-paying speaking engagements, reach key influencers in typically hard-to-reach places, and share our knowledge and expertise in bite-sized chunks of information that have the capacity to go viral in a *big* way.

The question isn't whether or not you should be on social media — that's a given if your target market frequents any digital network (and you'll know which one to use after having done your research on your ideal prospect); it's how to use these networks to distribute your information in a way that leads to direct sales, an online following and greater connection with your audience.

Forget what you've been taught about social media and content marketing, because this will smash it to pieces so you can start anew and establish online interactions that yield a six- to seven-figure revenue. And now that you know how to plan, package and produce content by using the Matrix Strategy of Content Creation from chapter 4, it's time to extend your reach in various ways by creating articles, videos, status updates and images that build your brand and market your message to assert your status and build your following. True to the Flee 9 to 5 lifestyle, of course, all of these tasks can be outsourced. Let's look deeper.

The hub technique: make social pay

Social media platforms are a traffic faucet—when it's on, it's on, but when a major player turns off the supply or redirects the pipes, revenues drop within minutes. Constantly changing algorithms and evolving platforms can put businesses at risk. For social to truly pay, your website must become the major *hub* for your audience so they are channeled back to it each and every time—like a major airport, if you will. It doesn't matter which platform you are using to share content such as articles, videos and status updates; all paths must lead back to you and directly into your ascension marketing model. Your prospects can opt in with an email address to further qualify, and you can collect the data and leads you need to be a success.

Email marketing humiliates social media in the conversion stakes. Consumers who receive email marketing spend 83 per cent more when shopping, and average a return on investment (ROI) of $44.25 for every dollar spent. But where does this traffic come from? A mix of banner advertising and publicity, direct promotions to other people's lists and, of course, social media. Although the conversion rates may not be on the 'front' end of this specific sales funnel, they certainly are on the back end.

Almost every social media post should in some way encourage users to go back to your website, where a purchase can be made and they can subscribe to receive future updates and promotions. This results in a higher quality list and higher future conversion rates, because users are being nurtured not only socially but via email and direct contact.

Frequency in exposure is key to a continual increase in revenue.

The reality is that Facebook, LinkedIn, Twitter, Instagram, Pinterest, Google+ or YouTube could change their algorithms at any moment, which in turn could dictate whether or not your social updates get seen in your fans' and followers' news feeds. The hub technique is like taking out an insurance policy on your future income. Social media platforms are just one of many channels in your ascension model and should never be relied upon solely.

Put your website at the centre of the social media universe simply by tagging a link back to it in 95 per cent or more of the posts you share online. If it goes viral, you'll benefit from the influx in traffic and subscribers. This is where the money is. Break these rules and you could go broke.

Although the network you use is important, what's also important is how you distribute your content throughout the various networks to gain fans and increase sales by creating momentum. I'll take a high-quality email list over a massive social-media fan base any day. And although I could delve into how to use each of these platforms now, you and I both know that that would be a futile exercise given the rate at which change occurs in social media. But what is even more important than the distribution network you use is *how* you choose to use it, because little changes can lead to big things.

The butterfly effect: distribute, share, shape

If a status update is posted online and nobody is around to read it, does it really exist? Surely for something to exist someone must have the ability to perceive it. Ideas need to be seen and heard and shared, and crafting these ideas into viral wins is much harder than many realise. With little tweaks along the way, though, you can create your own viral butterfly effect, by which small changes in one place result in large, often digitally instant differences somewhere else or some time down the track. And although different techniques are used on each platform, it always comes back to how you present your content, the type of content you share, when you post it, the frequency with which you share it, how you engage with and connect with your online audience, and the rate it grows.

There's a specific strategy that all agents of influence must follow to monetise their messages, and that is sharing extracts of their expertise with their target market through the social sphere. This is the content that upsells through your ascension marketing model before you even begin to worry about attracting fans, and that will make your competitors green with envy.

Take Elizabeth, for example. She has a 'principal product' that she would like to sell outside of her enlightened launch and evergreen campaigns to attract daily sales. It's a how-to program on getting a promotion at work. To sell it via social media Elizabeth would create free articles of 600 to 800 words or a five- to ten-minute video that shares the same framework as the content creation system. Limited by the length of article and video, she shares key points of her program. At the end of the video or article she will make her segue, just as she did with her 'introductory product': 'And, of course if you would love to learn more, click here to learn x, y and z.'

Elizabeth would distribute her article or video via all social media channels relevant to her specific target market in order to first establish credibility and naturally upsell the principal product. In doing this she creates another way to generate a consistent stream of revenue and growing engagement. How this content is created is just as important as the social channels it is marketed through. This content marketing specifically uses social media to drive a fan base and sales outcomes from which it can continue to grow.

Become an online giant through content marketing

Content marketing follows four distinct steps:

1 Create content (videos, articles, status updates, product extracts or free reports) that upsells a range of your products and establishes your credibility.

2 Promote this content through as many streams as possible, particularly social media. Keep it relevant so it doesn't have a short shelf-life and can be promoted month after month to leverage your way to profits.

3 Use social media to distribute it, and encourage engagement, liking and sharing of it to create social proof to further your goals and reach.

4 Build a social media following that fills your sales funnel day after day to syphon those leads across to your hub.

To begin, list 20 how-to article or video ideas for each of your proposed products, then cull them back to your top 10. Create the content for each one, providing a few gold nuggets, but ensuring the bulk of the 'gold' is to be sold in your primary product. Once your content is created it's time to distribute it, but before you do, arm yourself with product extracts — the next powerful component in your social media strategy.

Product extracts: one product, a thousand ways

Are you an industry leader? Prove it! Product extracts are simply a comment, sentence, thought or idea pulled from one of your primary products. For example:

> The quickest way to grow your business in 30 days or less is by employing a series of strategic marketing campaigns that build your profile, your business and your profits. Go here to learn more...

You do not mention the product itself, but you do mention the tool offered—'marketing campaigns' in this example. The great thing about the extract technique is that you can pull countless extracts from your products and never feel like you're promoting it the same way as before, so you can re-engage people who may have previously tuned out your ads. This allows you to prove your worth as an industry leader by giving people tidbits that set you apart from everyone else in your field. Include the landing page URL at the end of each extract. The length of the extract will be determined by the platform you post it to—for example, Facebook and LinkedIn can cope with longer ones, whereas Twitter must have a condensed version. One sentence to one paragraph is ideal. By following this process you'll identify 'breakaway' extracts that can later be used in advertising copy because they have been proven to work. This style is one of my favourites, because you can attract comments and create a conversation around the extract, instead of always pushing your products directly.

The biggest social media marketing mistake ever

This content will not only be used to upsell into your ascension marketing model and fill your funnel; when it measures up against my 'engagement ruler', which I'll get to shortly, it will also be leveraged to attract a solid base of fans and followers who stalk your every move. But before I get to that, it's key to understand the biggest social media mistake everyone seems to make: promoting content via your channels only once!

There isn't one way to promote one product; there are thousands of ways, just as there are thousands of ways to promote an article or video via social media, particularly more than once on the same social media channels. Each piece of content, specifically articles and videos, should enjoy a solid campaign that aims to reach out to as many individuals as possible within that time frame to help attract more fans and prospects. This can be achieved in a number of ways:

- You can post a link to the content each day, Monday through Friday, but in different formats. For example, it can be posted with a quote from the article/video and a link to read/watch more.

- You can change the headline of the content to test and measure which one gets the greatest number of click-throughs back to your site, and rerun it periodically.

- You can post an image with the content or just promote it with plain text.

- Again, you can repurpose this content into different formats and re-release it at various times throughout the year to maximise its reach and your sales and minimise your workload.

It's critical to understand that our social media followings can grow by hundreds each day. These individuals won't be exposed to your older content unless you direct them to it. It gets lost and buried in the news feed. This is part of your social media schedule and can re-engage individuals who may have lost interest at some point. It can also be achieved by running Flashback Fridays or Throwback Thursdays intermittently throughout the year.

Remember the agent's mantra: create it once, leverage it forever.

Take a look at this sample schedule of social media posts.

The 7-day social media posting cycle: how to create a social media schedule

Where many businesses fall flat is in relying on ad hoc efforts at engagement through their social media posts. A consistent schedule will ensure you attract and keep the engagement of your online following. It is critical to test and measure it to get the best result. Some markets will be more active at particular times of the day than at others. Using a tool such as Bitly (www.bit.ly.com) to track your website's specific URL hits via social media enables you to see which posts were better received than others, and when. Test the following:

- *Morning vs afternoon and later posts.* Re-post a link to an article in the middle of the night for your overseas audiences.

- *Video vs articles.* Test the different formats to see which one specifically appeals to your audience.

- *Platform effectiveness.* Compare Google+, Facebook, Twitter, Instagram, Pinterest, LinkedIn and more. Be sure to research Google+, as its relevance in ranking your website will be critical in the digital world in the coming years.

- *Conversion rates.* Each platform will result in different conversion rates. Test it, track it and rework your campaigns to continually increase your sales and profit margins.

Begin by mapping out a seven-day schedule using the suggestions in table 7.1 (overleaf), knowing that by outsourcing to a copywriter this process can suddenly become easy and seamless.

Table 7.1: the 7-day social media posting cycle (*example*)

Post	Sunday	Monday	Tuesday	Wednesday	Thursday	Friday	Saturday
Inspirational quote (your own or someone else's)	×1						
Product extract		×1			×1		
Picture quote			×1	×1			
Article link (same article, varying headlines, all platforms)		×1	×1				
Video post (same video promoted 3 times)					×1	×1	×1
Introductory offer	×1						
Share a resource (share a link to another resource your audience will find interesting/ engaging; twice per week maximum)							×1
Client case study or testimonial			×1				
Q&A session or multiple choice (keep topic in alignment with articles/ videos being promoted that week for maximum exposure and engagement)		×1	×1				

Visit www.benangel.com.au/flee9-5 for a downloadable template to fill out.

As you can see, in the example in table 7.1 there are 17 posts within a seven-day period that engage your audience using different media and styles of communication — all of which can be scheduled in advance using a VA. Ideally, use as many of your own quotes as possible, not other people's thoughts. We want your channel to be 'clean', focusing on the core messages you share with your audience to help you lead your tribe and achieve success.

'Show me your teeth, little monsters!' — Lady Gaga

For all her controversy, Lady Gaga is one of the smartest marketers of our time. Her first tour to Australia saw her bring a 5-metre-high 'monster' out on stage. Midway through her performance she screamed out at the top of her lungs, 'To kill the monster … you have to take its picture!' My friend and I turned to look at each other in awe — she was driving a social media revolution by encouraging thousands of her fans to take pictures of her, of course encouraging them to share these images on social media. Given her following of more than 60 million, it's hard to dispute the savvy behind such a simple but powerful ploy to drive real-world engagement online. Think creatively and be rewarded.

Lead the tribe or get lost in the news feed

A tribe is a group of people connected to one another, connected to a leader, and connected to an idea. For millions of years, human beings have been part of one tribe or another. A group needs only two things to be a tribe: a shared interest and a way to communicate.
— **Seth Godin, *Tribes: We Need You to Lead Us***

Social media has given us the capacity to be the master of our tribe from anywhere in the world, and being that master means one thing and one thing only — you must lead it. But before you can lead you must cultivate your tribe of online followers by learning how to successfully engage them. Without this engagement any effort to build your fan base will be in vain, which is why engagement is the first critical step and attracting fans is the second. If you already have a tribe, these strategies will help you push past any plateau in growth you may have experienced of late and immediately attract more fans to your media pages. And if you're just getting started, you'll have an unbeatable strategy with which to arm yourself.

We lead our tribes by using the engagement ruler as our guide.

Going viral with the social media engagement ruler (ER)

For successful engagement we need the ability to stir emotion and inspire thought, and, most importantly, to incite action. If we can't do this, we miss the mark and our reach is far from what we need it to be. This applies not only to social media, but to all the content you create and the conversations you have. When creating content, measure it on the ER to test how effective it will be online and whether or not it has the ability to go viral.

Content can be classified into three types: conflict, neutrality and elation. Let's take a look at each one.

ER #1: Conflict

Creating inner conflict in social media can have massive payoffs, particularly when it is centred on your topic. Conflict can be achieved by discussing the 'elephant in the room' — the subject that no other agents want to touch because it's too controversial. When handled well, however, opening up these subjects to social media scrutiny can immediately polarise your audience and allow you to solidify and lead a tribe of loyal followers while the others fall by the wayside. Think now of the 'elephant in the room' in your industry, the topic that no one wants to discuss, yet if you did, it could transform lives. For example:

- Is depression a 'choice' or is it a chemical imbalance?
- Which weight loss programs can create a health risk?

To be recognised as an agent you must have a firm opinion. Not everyone is going to agree with you. Thankfully that's not the goal, or we would never be able to generate conversations that provoke change in the world. Find out what your audience's greatest fears, needs and wants are, and discuss them openly. This could even spawn a new product category and fill a void within your niche. Propose it in the form of questions, opinions, articles and videos, and watch the conversation spark on your fan pages. This point on the engagement ruler is massively viral and can help to attract international media coverage.

ER #2: Neutrality

In the middle of the ER is neutrality. Neutral engagement has little to no impact. It doesn't compel, nor does it conflict — it just is. This style of content may garner 'likes', but it is highly unlikely to go viral or get shared. While this may present solid educational value, it will not compel people to take action to follow your social media pages or sign up on your website. Still, it is a necessary part of the mix of content posted.

ER #3: Elation

Passion is a fantastic driving force to get people to like, share and buy. Show your passion to create elation through your status updates, articles and videos. Add your personality to the mix to lift it up to an entirely new level, one that your competitors can't compete with. You're presenting the same information but saying it in a new and refreshing way that makes you aspirational and appeals to our primal instincts.

Getting the right mix

Great (not good) social media posts oscillate between these three points on the spectrum. The trick is to strategically pick which one you will use at any given time, thereby optimising your social reach. Next time you see a quote, picture or video being shared online, see if you can pick at which point on the ER that engagement sits and why it has or has not been successful. By observing, you will begin to adapt your social media marketing style in a direction that ensures you will build a massive online following.

Test your content now against the engagement ruler illustrated in table 7.2. Where would your most recent social media status update sit, even if you simply shared someone else's post?

Table 7.2: the engagement ruler (ER)

1. Conflict 0–4	2. Neutrality 5	3. Elation 6–10
Polarising	Neither happy nor sad	Funny
Thought-provoking	Just 'is'	Passionate
Angering	Lack of action	Exuberant
Saddening	No momentum	Inspires
Depressing		Motivates
		Creates momentum

Engage your tribe and your tribe will engage your services.

The strategy: move fast, move often and move minds

Now you are clear on how to engage a fan base, it's time to attract and build one. I'll now share with you strategies that will stand the test of time and the impact of any new platform the IT gods decide to throw at us in the coming years. You'll want to adapt each of these strategies in varying ways and at various times, depending on your focus after you have filled out the 3X Customer Formula (see p. 51), located which channels your prospects frequent and set up your social media pages. But I'll now present the essence of each. This will also help you overcome any social media inertia you might experience.

I follow the golden rule: move fast, move often and move minds.

This is key in attracting a new fan base and re-igniting an existing one. You don't have to be the first to market in your industry. In fact, being first is rarely a good idea, because you have to run a major campaign to first educate people about your new niche and then 'sell' them on the concept. But you do have to have a consistent presence, which can be fully automated by your VAs.

Step 1 is to set up the social media pages you would like to focus on now and throw your full weight behind each one; step 2 is to run campaigns such as these to attract your tribe:

- *Existing networks*. After you have encouraged your existing professional and personal networks to opt into your hub, invite them to your social channels. Send a minimum of three invitations to each one.

- *External networks*. Ask your existing network to send an invitation to their networks to extend your reach. Offer a prize for the most referrals (or new fans, followers or subscribers) to your social channels.

- *Social media cross-promotion*. Partner up with businesses that offer products and services that are complementary to yours. Send out emails to one another's social channels and email lists encouraging one another's networks to become fans. Once again, offer some kind of incentive—for example, the 500th person to 'like' your page will receive a copy of your book or primary product.

- *Run a competition*. On sites such as Facebook you can run competitions using third-party apps that encourage people to become a fan and share the competition details in order to win a prize. Generally speaking, a game of skill (that is, where people submit an entry and you judge the winner) is easier and cheaper to run than a game of chance (that is, a random draw). This is because in some places (such as NSW in Australia for example) a government permit is required to run a competition that involves a random draw. Check the legal rules that might be applicable to the competition you wish to run before you run it. Also check the relevant terms and conditions on the social media channel to ensure you adhere to their policies.

- *Nominate your local hero competition*. Leverage not only social media but mainstream media to nominate a 'local hero' who deserves to win one of your products. This can create an enormous amount of goodwill on your channel.

- *Run a 72-hour Q&A session on your Facebook feed.* This is one of my favourite strategies. I will answer as many questions as I can on a specific topic within the defined time. Promote this to your email list and through your other networks, sending them directly to the post where they can put their question. Offer sample questions for them to ask. You'll find the questions you are asked can be adapted into other content that can be featured later. It also offers a fantastic opportunity to upsell your products. A recent one I ran attracted over 100 comments within three days and resulted in direct sales.

- *Hit Like/Share/Hashtag posts.* Depending on our personal settings, generally when we like, share or hashtag a social media post, that information is shared to our personal and/or professional networks, thus reaching a larger audience. Run a post such as: 'Hit Like if you're excited about the weekend'. This formula can be used in various formats ('Hit Share if you love social media', and so on). Encourage people to engage and they'll be more likely to like, share or hashtag future posts.

- *Use events to drive fans.* Use actual events, as Gaga did (see p. 123), to drive fans to your social media pages. This could be a Google+ hangout session, webinar, live speaking engagement or publicity expo. Tie in a competition to social media to reach more prospects and drive them online.

You will have noticed that I have left advertising directly to fans off this list. Why? Because, as we've discussed, as much as possible they need to go straight to your hub and then on to social media to help speed up cash flow and increase profits. This is always objective number one. Objective number two is to increase your fan base, leveraging their networks on social media using a mix of the strategies outlined — a winning combination if ever there was one.

Set, but don't forget

Lastly, but most importantly, although you will have established your social media schedule, maybe outsourced the production of the specific content to a skilled copywriter and got a VA to schedule your updates to appear automatically, you will still need to check in and proactively engage with the interactions that occur. This will help you keep your finger on the pulse and immediately respond to any queries or challenges that come up, or assign a team member to manage them.

These strategies are designed to monetise social media in a way few companies have been able to achieve in recent years. For updates on specific training programs on any of the platforms mentioned in this chapter, you know the drill: visit www.benangel.com.au/flee9-5.

Now it's time to go back to New York—to uncover how to create international reach in innovative ways.

Tips and resources

→ A good email marketing campaign is far more profitable than a massive social media fan base, but with careful, strategic content marketing you can build a social media following that will keep your sales funnel filled indefinitely.

→ Your website must become the major hub for your audience so they are channeled back to it every time; all paths must lead back directly to your ascension marketing model.

→ Cultivate your tribe of online followers by learning how to successfully engage them using the engagement ruler — then lead them.

Visit www.benangel.com.au/flee9-5 for a downloadable template of the 7-day social media posting cycle, and for updates on specific training programs on any of the platforms mentioned in this chapter.

8 PUBLICITY
The master media manipulators

→ How I secured an $80 000 contract from one article

I always have a full-length mirror next to the camera when I'm doing publicity stills. That way, I know how I look.
— **Marilyn Monroe**

How do tens of thousands of experts and their businesses come to be featured in countless publications and on TV and radio shows every year, becoming the go-to experts within their fields?

Many believe, 'So long as your business is unique, that's what's important!' But how many do you know who have unique stories that go unnoticed, unrecognised — and unpaid? Some say, 'It takes expensive publicists with influential contacts, and I'll never have the funds to employ them'. I'm here to tell you that these people are wrong.

You can start from scratch and still succeed.

In walked the media

After a few short hours of broken sleep I made my way through Times Square to the Hotel Pennsylvania on 7th Avenue, opposite Madison Square Garden. It could have been a hotel out of a horror movie. Four American flags rippled in the breeze between the grand columns of its looming facade. Its hallways were filled with Art Deco paintings and fixtures.

The media contingent filed into the vast conference room on the top floor of the hotel, taking their seats before the long tables that spread from stage left to right, as if at a world summit waiting to pledge their allegiance to their country. There were producers from *The View*, *Good Morning America*, *Today* and Fox News, journalists and editors from *Fast Company* and *Time* magazine, and representatives from at least three prominent publishing houses. It was Steve Harrison's National Publicity Summit, which brought together a select group of media players twice a year.

I sat in the audience ready to take notes as if they were about to spew forth gold. Each of them had 120 seconds to tell us precisely how they wanted us to pitch to them in the breakout sessions we were to attend later. Here each of us would have just 60 seconds to make an impression that could potentially win us international coverage.

Face time with these players offered participants a chance to take an unknown brand into the stratosphere, to influence a country, or destroy the brand in one fell swoop. These people had audiences ranging from one million to over three million viewers per day. This wasn't the little leagues. It was time to play with the big boys and girls in the field, to step up or go home.

Unleash the agent globally: why you need publicity — and fast

Publicity is one of the fastest and most affordable ways for an agent of influence to get their message out into the marketplace and dramatically boost their sales. It doesn't matter what your message is, where you live in the world or what product you have, there are thousands of opportunities for you to make your mark and leverage your time. Publicity — marketing in ways that can shape careers overnight and change lives — is one of the critical strategies we have covered in previous chapters.

As we saw with Rhonda Byrne and *The Secret*, it can instantly put your products and services, and you yourself, in front of millions of prospective customers. The boost to your credibility can then be leveraged to help increase your online conversion rates instantly. A short interview conducted over the telephone or using Skype, needing little preparation, can be worth tens of thousands of dollars in sales and coverage. This is the essence of the Flee 9 to 5 message: it maximises time and reach for revenue no matter where you live.

In this chapter I will let you inside the dark and manipulative world of the media, and teach you how, with little effort and time, you can use it to your advantage — to put you in front of your prospective clients weekly on a mass scale. I'll share with you my own unique experiences, from being on both sides of the camera and the interview chair, as a host and a columnist, to working with insider contacts in TV, radio and print who have shared with me the inner workings of the game, right through to pitching to some of the biggest media in the world. Stories of success and, of course, of failure too.

The great news is that you don't have to spend countless hours writing press releases or making endless phone calls. I'll set you on the right path, so that after you take a few simple but critical steps towards making your personal brand magnetic, it will be the media who will be contacting you.

But before we get to that, let's take a look at our six core objectives for the next step in our journey together.

Six reasons why the mainstream media is critical to your success

Credibility is a basic survival tool.
— Rebecca Solnit

Having successfully secured publicity for my clients in media as diverse as *The Huffington Post, Vogue, Marie Claire, CLEO, The Sydney Morning Herald, Woman's Day* and *The Herald Sun*, as well as with countless TV and radio shows, magazines and prominent blogs internationally, I know what it takes to get publicity and I know what it can do for an up-and-coming agent of influence. There are many reasons why getting media coverage is critical, but none is more important than the following six reasons.

1. Instant credibility: skip to the head of the line

Like a university degree, media coverage can provide credibility. If a producer, editor or journalist is willing to feature someone in their publication or on their show in front of hundreds of thousands, if not millions, then they already perceive that person as having credibility. I have seen publicity fast-track careers, help secure book deals and paid speaking engagements, boost sales and create public profiles that can then be leveraged to launch a person's next big career move, or indeed allow them to take time off to focus on other passions. Just one feature column, appearance or interview can change everything in hours — not days, weeks, months or even years.

2. Increased conversion rates: improve your profits

Any media coverage obtained can be featured across your products, blog, social media pages and websites, and automatically translates into an increase in conversion rates — in many cases upwards of 5 per cent, which we now know is a lot in online marketing. It ultimately influences purchasing decisions, especially for people who are undecided on whether or not to proceed to your online shopping cart. This exposure sets you apart from other experts in your field. It takes you to the front of the line, skipping past your competitors, who will be wondering where the hell you came from. And believe me, getting good coverage can be a challenge, but only when you don't know what you're doing.

3. Spread the word: build your following en masse

Just like social media, by tying mainstream media coverage back to your website and social media channels you can quickly feed thousands of new prospects into your ascension marketing model for free. In each media interview you do, if possible always mention that there are free resources available on your website. Some media outlets will allow you to do this; others may not, but there is no harm in trying. If you don't ask, you don't get — it's that simple.

4. Speaking engagements: share your message on stage

One of the major benefits of being an agent of influence is being invited to speak at events and getting paid for doing what you love — upwards of $2000 in many cases. Top speakers and high-profile individuals can command anywhere from $50 000 to $100 000 or more — a big incentive to work and play in this amazing space. Getting media coverage for your brand helps to capture the attention of conference organisers and CEOs who run regular events in which you can extend your reach and your message and connect directly with your fan base. Two prominent millionaires I work with continue to use this as a strategy from time to time to reconnect with their audience and create a buzz in the 'real world' as well as the digital one, and to drive a dramatic boost in sales and exposure. And each new presentation you make is also a potential product. You get paid not only to speak in front of an audience but also to create new content. Win–win.

5. Endorsement deals: get paid to promote

Over the years, I have leveraged my profile to secure free filming, websites, venue hire, photographic packages, clothes and, yes, even free laser hair treatments! (FYI, I no longer look like Chewbacca!) And, if you're starting out on a budget, know that not having a massive lump sum to invest to get started is not an excuse to fall behind in the progress department; rather, it is a reason to look for other, more creative ways to make it work.

Don't say no, ask how.

Just as you are looking for a break to gain greater exposure, remind yourself that others are doing the same. Teaming up with high-profile individuals and companies gives you an opportunity to attract endorsement deals and break through doors that would otherwise be closed to you. It gives you bargaining power to take the next big step up. Think about other businesses within your industry that offer complementary products and services, and how you could both benefit from teaming up in new and creative ways to reach your audiences together.

6. Increase what you charge and attract high-paying clients

In marketing, perception is everything, and to be successful you must manipulate and manage how you are perceived in the marketplace, because if you don't, others will. One piece of publicity can be utilised to increase what you charge — particularly for services. Strategically mentioning specific media coverage throughout presentations, products, press releases and social media helps shape the way you are perceived. One article I wrote for a little-known business magazine a while ago resulted in my securing an international contract with a remote client worth over $80 000, for less than ten hours of telephone and/or email consulting per month for one year — all from a piece that took me less than two hours to write. Remember, it's not what you charge, it's the value that you provide that makes the difference — and how you demonstrate that value publicly so people know you're the go-to person in your industry. A little article for a small audience can result in a big payoff.

Never underestimate media coverage — it will surprise you every time.

Brand revolution: crafting the celebrity brand that pays

A definitive moment in my career was when I changed my website image from a boring profile shot to one in which I had my top off, a noticeably raised eyebrow, and masking tape over my mouth with the words 'limited edition' written on it. Within a few days my subscriber list grew dramatically, and within three short months I had been approached by three TV producers.

Why? Because the image successfully communicated a side of my personality that could not be captured in a conventional image, and it aligned with my personal brand and values of being adventurous, daring and groundbreaking.

You can use your own visual imagery as a catalyst to transform your career.

Every agent must have an image that stands out and grabs people's attention in a way that is well thought-out and, more importantly, well executed. It is about expressing your internal world externally, and when the two align, absolutely nothing can stop you. Your brand becomes magnetic. This alignment immediately piques people's interest and garners new attention.

Now, do you have to take your top off? No! But you do need to think of an edgy way to get your message across through your images. It is the 'packaged you' that gets presented to the media. You are packaging the intangible, the essence of who you are — a version of you that has mass appeal and that is potentially polarising but also eye-catching. Without this imagery, the task of getting publicity suddenly becomes much harder, especially on visual platforms like TV, print and online. This image will not only express who you are but convey your brand message, which will help your tribe find and connect with you.

For example, when working with Leon and Patrick Harvey from Sukkie — a more tooth-friendly sports drink — we were able to push the boundaries in significant ways. I suggested the idea of a picture of Leon suited up as an entrepreneur squeezing a bottle of raspberry-flavoured Sukkie all over himself, against a bright white backdrop so the product and Leon popped. The image immediately captures one's attention and the spirit of a groundbreaking brand that is entering a competitive market without the millions in backing that larger competitors like Gatorade have. It's not about the money. It's about ideas that can shift perception and capture audiences in new, unexpected and fun ways — even if you are on a budget.

In our very first conversation Danette, the former Oprah producer, said to me after having a look at my website, 'Ben, you meet the criteria a great producer looks for: (1) you're interesting, (2) we can see where you fit and (3) you look great on camera'. It was something I'd worked for years to achieve: a groomed, amplified version of myself that connects.

The three pillars of PR success: the breakdown

Let's delve into each of these components in depth now.

1. Become interesting

Almost every day I come across individuals who are apologising for who they are simply through the way they stand and speak and stay out of the limelight. And, if you have the personality of a toaster, we have a problem. To be a stand-out in the media, you need to be a stand-out in your own eyes. Whether you're an introvert or an extrovert is irrelevant; these skills can be taught and groomed. It's not about being arrogant, it's about being self-assured, secure in the knowledge that you know your stuff, and if there are gaps in your education you immediately know how to fill them. This helps to build confidence and draw out the 'interesting' aspects of your true personality that you may have been too afraid to share because of a fear of being judged.

Being 'interesting' is at the heart of winning publicity. The media is forever seeking interesting people and stories — stories that you can comment on as an expert in your field. And it's not just about the story, it's also about the angle and the specific media that take up the idea. Matching an interesting personality with an interesting story makes for a winning combination that many have found hard to achieve, until now.

What can you discuss in the media?

To start, reverse engineer. Look at the core product or service you generate most of your profits from, identify its core message, then create stories associated with this message to take to the media. For example, Melissa is a hypnotist. One of her products helps with weight loss. The core message, or 'tool' if you like, is hypnotherapy, which can be applied to weight loss. This linkage presents a potential news story. It also guarantees that there's a direct tie-in with your product or service to help drive sales, instead of a haphazard attempt at getting publicity.

It also helps you become 'known' quickly as an expert in a specific area. Once you've identified your core message or tool, identify the types of topics in your area of expertise that you can discuss in the media. Think for a moment. Can you comment on any of the following within your industry?

- the release of a groundbreaking product or service, and why it's going to transform your industry

- solutions to a negative news story

- an event that involves a charity

- commentary on a breaking political or celebrity story

- the introduction of an unpopular approach to an old problem

- rising above adversity (Be your own case study: how did you overcome a personal or professional challenge, and how can you share this knowledge with the rest of the world? This then feeds into your ascension marketing model. Tie it in with a breaking news topic to make it immediately relevant.)

- the industry elephant in the room that nobody is willing to talk about

- top tips that can help a media audience solve a common problem.

And that's just the beginning. Next we take the idea and make it more interesting by packaging it using a few keywords to capture the media's interest. But first ...

Who's on your media hit list?

Before we package it, it's time to do some research. Which media platform would gain you the greatest amount of exposure in front of your specific target audience? Now create what I call 'your media hit list' of the top 10 publications, TV or radio shows, blogs or online media that would best help you achieve your objective.

This one step will save you a lot of time later and immediately position you for greater success. Why? Because you're instantly relevant to them! They're used to covering stories within your niche, which makes you a perfect candidate for future features, because you're a natural fit. In other words, don't try to cram a square peg into a round hole, which is what 99 per cent of people do.

Once you've identified your list, it's time to watch, read or listen to each one to find out how they position their story ideas, because now it's time to package yours.

What will you pitch?

Let's say you've completed your homework, which shouldn't take you more than an hour or so to refine (if you haven't already done so). It's now time to create a pitch or write a press release. Tragically this is where many get stuck...

Personally I find this the most exciting part of gaining media coverage. Your pitch will be a very short email (usually under 300 words), in which you will sell a media producer or editor a story idea or something you could comment on, or provide additional resources for an article or segment idea they might feature. In a press release this idea will be developed and distributed via email to the wider media, including through online channels such as www.prweb.com. A mix of both types of communication will ensure all bases are covered. To get a free press release template and to find out more on how you can get your hands on media contact lists to help make it easy to get your pitches and releases in front of top producers, editors and journalists, visit www.benangel.com.au/flee9-5.

Because the press release is simply an expanded version of a pitch written in an email, we will focus first on how to come up with a winning formula. Base your own pitches and releases on the formula your targeted media use.

This 'formula' will include the writing style and conventions adopted by a particular media outlet — for example, the way it uses headlines that draw large audiences to its network or publication. It's often the headlines on the front of the magazine that help it to sell millions of copies. They are well researched -- nothing is left to chance. To help come up with fresh new ideas so you can see how a formula is created, check out these fill-in-the-blank formula ideas.

Six publicity formulas you can use to help you get more media coverage

1 When _____ happens, could you _____?
(for example, 'When illness happens, could you still pay the rent?')

2 Does your _____ need_____?
(for example, 'Does your image need help?')

3 Could you _____ and _____?
(for example, 'Could you give it all away and still survive?')

4 Surveys show that _____ is stronger than _____.
(for example, 'Surveys show that the fear of loss is stronger than the lure of profit.')

5 Here's how to get _____ and _____.
(for example, 'Here's how to get out of your slump and into your shine.')

6 Have _____ become _____?
(for example, 'Have pets become fashion accessories?')

As you can see, such headlines are short, punchy and straight to the point, and they can help you get your foot in the door. I have a huge list of formula ideas I refer to regularly that helps me come up with pitch ideas and headings for press releases at a moment's notice. Remember, timing is everything in the media and in most instances, if you don't provide your commentary on a breaking news story within the first few hours, you've missed the boat. You can turn your headline into a brief email pitch or write a press release based on the topic.

Using the formulas I've listed as models, start to formulate ideas that you could take to the media. Next, think about the personality you bring to the mix. The consistent advice I've received from media people in all fields is, 'Just be yourself'. It rings like a mantra in this area, being repeated over and over again, until … one day it finally *clicks* and sinks in. While we do need to groom ourselves for the media we are approaching, it is when we bring our own personality and a new angle to an old subject that things begin to fall into place and pick up pace. Being yourself in the public eye takes practice, but I'll get into that in the next chapter.

2. How you fit: stereotype yourself before you get typecast

> *In real life, I'm not super-posh but if that's the stereotype,*
> *I really don't care. It could be worse.*
> — **Sophie Ellis-Bextor**

We've all been taught that it's rude to stereotype others and place them in a box. But if the media can't stereotype you and work out where you fit in their publication, show or news story, in their eyes you won't belong in their world. If you do not stereotype yourself, the media will surely typecast you … if you can get that far in the first place. The media must identify you in a story or article by your role or title, in order to place you in 'context' so that the audience will understand why you're commenting on it; otherwise your involvement in the story or feature does not make sense.

When approaching the media, clearly identify yourself as a particular expert within a particular field. My client Dr Rebecca Harwin is an expert on polycystic ovarian syndrome (PCOS). This unique niche has secured her coverage in magazines from *Vogue* and *Women's Health* right through to the *Body & Soul* lift-out of a major Australian newspaper. Let's begin now:

How do you want the media to introduce you? For example:

- 'Dale Freemantle, a prominent sales expert, says …'
- 'Melanie Jacobs, a leading hypnotherapist, says …'

Now it's your turn.

'_____ [name], a _____, says …'

When my clients have stereotyped themselves it immediately changes market perceptions of them: they become 'known' for and linked to something specific, which leads to paid speaking engagements, online product sales and high-paid consulting projects, from which they can pick and choose because they are suddenly in demand. This is the first step in manipulating the media for your cause. You need to take the first step — before you fall victim to their typecasting.

3. How you look: look the part or lose the part

The secret to modeling is not being perfect. What one needs is a face that people can identify in a second. You have to be given what's needed by nature, and what's needed is to bring something new.
— **Karl Lagerfeld**

So you've positioned yourself for success by way of the topics you can discuss in the media and the unique and interesting personality and ideas you bring to your topic, along with knowing how to stereotype yourself so you find a place in the media landscape. Now we have to look at how you're visually packaged. Images needed to get copious amounts of coverage to pique the interest of key influencers include:

- interesting, high-quality pictures of you, as the expert in your field, that bring out your personality

- short (three- to four-minute) video clips in which you're speaking straight to camera or being interviewed on your subject of expertise

- an online media page that includes your video content, images, past media coverage and possible story ideas.

The three tools we've discussed help the media immediately position you in their publication or on their show, where you can demonstrate your knowledge and look great on camera. The golden rule is if you don't look like what you do, no one will trust you and the media, as well as potential clients, will overlook you. Look like the expert you are and the media will feature you as the expert you are. You are interview ready.

For tips on dressing for your industry, get your free copy of *Sleeping Your Way to The Top in Business* by visiting www .benangel.com.au.

Her own brother arranged the murder of her mother: when *not* to share your story publicly

Rhondalynn Korolak, with whom I had the pleasure of working some years ago, approached me regarding a very sensitive topic. You see, her own brother had promised three 16-year-old boys a beat-up $500 truck as a reward if they murdered his and Rhondalynn's mother. The boys went to her house in the middle of the night and brutally murdered her as promised. Rhondalynn had shared this story in her book, *On The Shoulders of Giants*, but had yet to speak about it openly in the media. She asked me if I thought it was appropriate. I replied, 'Only you know when you're ready to share that story. But understand, a story like yours can transform lives and help thousands, because it reveals your courage in stepping up and shows that anyone can overcome anything that life throws at them with the time and the tools to heal'.

A few short weeks later, Rhondalynn decided to share her story. A major Australian magazine did a phenomenal feature on her that instantly helped to put many individuals' problems into perspective.

If you're going to share your story and it happens to be incredibly sensitive, wait until you are in a place where you are strong enough to talk about it publicly. If you become too upset, instead of feeling inspired by you, people will feel sorry for you, which is not the desired outcome for an aspirational leader. Revealing vulnerability is fantastic, but only in small doses.

I was flat-out rejected!

I'd just pitched to the producer of *The View*, one of America's biggest daytime talk shows, which then featured Barbara Walters, Whoopi Goldberg, Joy Behar and Elisabeth Hasselbeck. He spoke faster than all of the women combined and even with my five-hour energy drink I was scarcely able to keep up, given it was now 3 am back home in Melbourne, Australia.

But this wasn't going to stop me. I mean, what's the worst that could happen? I could be rejected by one of the biggest TV producers in the world. Oh wait, it just did happen. And, well, it wasn't that bad.

In that moment I decided to march right up to a publisher who was also at the conference. I gave him a 20-second pitch just as he was about to leave … a pitch that many months later would change my life.

Tips and resources

→ Publicity is one of the fastest and most affordable ways to get your message out into the marketplace and dramatically boost sales; handled well, it can change your life overnight.

→ Use your own visual imagery as a catalyst to convey your brand message, help your tribe find and connect with you, and transform your career.

→ Remember the three pillars of PR success: be an interesting personality with an interesting story to tell; stereotype yourself so the media can see where you fit and the value you can offer them; look the part by packaging yourself in a credible and engaging way.

For a press release template and more on media contact lists, visit www.benangel.com.au/flee9-5. For tips on dressing for your industry, pick up a free copy of my *Sleeping Your Way to The Top in Business* by visiting www.benangel.com.au.

---

9 THE CRITICS
Public and private
enemy number one

→ You're shaping the world, not
   remodelling your bathroom

> *You have enemies? Good. That means you've*
> *stood up for something, sometime in your life.*
> — **Winston Churchill**

The National Hurricane Centre reported that Hurricane Sandy's tropical-force winds extended 820 miles (more than 1300 kilometres) at their widest. In the US the storm took 125 lives, wiping out power and communications to half of Manhattan and a reported 7.5 million people. New Jersey was the worst hit. The damage bill was second only to Hurricane Katrina's.

Alex and I were in Greenwich Village, safe in an old New York apartment building watching the coverage on NY1. I instantly recognised the reporter. It was Cheryl Wills, the second person I'd met at the publicity summit. She was reporting on the collapse of a crane atop a Manhattan high-rise on West 57th Street. The front of one building had collapsed and the crane still perched precariously many storeys above the street. The street would remain cordoned off for another week until they worked out how to get it down. The surrounding buildings had been evacuated, including the hotel I'd found myself in on my second night in the city.

Halfway through Cheryl's report the power went down. That's when it sunk in. Sandy was here. 'Happy Halloween', we wished each other. We played Uno in the dark on my iPad until the battery died. That night I went off the grid.

The next morning we surveyed the damage while on a mission. Along with a hundred other New Yorkers who didn't know what to do until they'd had their caffeine fix, Alex *had* to find a coffee. There was major flooding a few blocks over from us. We found ourselves in lower Manhattan at the start of what would be more than seven days without power, and with a cold snap fast approaching. We had to make plans fast.

The darkened city would experience a sharp rise in burglaries and sexual assaults, along with food and fuel shortages. Mayor Bloomberg limited access to the city to cars with three or more passengers — the rest were turned away. Without streetlights there were few cars on the road. We were asked to share cabs to save fuel.

For the next week we bathed in water that we heated on the gas stovetop that was thankfully still connected. The first night we used the only candle we had been able to find after hours of searching, at Duane & Reade in Times Square. Cinnamon scented. The scent now repulses me.

The second night, using a phone to light our way, Alex and I climbed the narrow staircase to the roof of the apartment building. It was an eerie sight: while the lower part of the island was plunged in darkness, to the north it was lit up like a Christmas tree — including the Empire State Building and Times Square in the distance. Around us the usual hum of the city, dominated by air conditioning units, endless traffic, trains and sirens, was virtually silenced. One of the busiest cities in the world had been brought to its knees.

The $10 000 I'd spent to get here and the 70 pitches I'd made to some of the world's top media were all forgotten now, wiped from the page in one fell swoop. All attention had turned to the hurricane, and rightly so. Half of the media people lived on Manhattan, and some were also responsible for getting the news out to people who needed help the most.

It was going to take alcohol, resilience, friendship and distractions to see us through this mess. I was going to be stuck here for another week. Wifi, accessed through Starbuck's window, was to become a close companion, as it was for many other tourists and New Yorkers who pressed up against the glass as they tried to work out their next moves.

When life happens, it really happens.

The enemy without: what no one ever talks about, but should!

> *To avoid criticism say nothing, do nothing, be nothing.*
> — **Aristotle**

There are two kinds of enemies we must deal with in our lives — the enemies within and the enemies without. Among the enemies without are people, circumstances, scenarios and beliefs that can take our power away from us and momentarily throw us off track, if we allow them to. Life happens (and hurricanes happen), and things get in the way, but it's how you deal with it and refocus that matters. As an agent of influence, you're going to have many enemies in your lifetime, including your own thoughts. People will disagree with your opinions and criticise your work (reading these pages will certainly provoke internal criticism among some readers). Internal and external doubts are all part of the same evolutionary process that we must each go through to fulfil our vision. It's only natural.

Everyone with a name in this world has their critics, who will try to tear them down and take away their right to voice their opinion on whatever it is that they find important, even the so-called mundane. And since you are here to shape the world we live in, and not just to remodel your bathroom and fit in with the crowd, it's important for me to share with you some important stories that no one ever talks about, but should — the elephant in the room, if you like.

Through these pages I've shown you how to draw out your passion and turn it into profit and attract mass exposure when applied as planned. It would be remiss of me not to also show you how to handle your critics as you progress throughout your career — along with your own inner critic, who at times can become your private enemy number one.

And no matter how successful you are in creating a fulfilling lifestyle business that shapes thoughts, opinions and behaviours, you will have your naysayers. It's part of the game — you just have to learn how to play it strategically.

While social media has given us powerful communication tools, it has also provided users with the weapons to criticise and do harm. I know this well.

Annah makes headlines — for all the wrong reasons

Let me never fall into the vulgar mistake of dreaming that I am persecuted whenever I am contradicted.
— **Ralph Waldo Emerson,** *Emerson in His Journals*

'We'll do whatever it takes to bring you to your knees!' was one threat made to my client Annah Stretton, a high-profile New Zealand fashion designer. The day before, a picture of Annah on a bearskin rug (complete with taxidermied head) with her two pet pooches went public. In the story Annah professed to support animal rights. It was a contradiction in message that even Annah publicly acknowledged. It was an oversight. The rug itself had been purchased after an officially sanctioned cull in a Canadian national park as a result of overpopulation. The certificate to this effect wasn't good enough.

A flood of outrage ensued, first hitting her social media page that afternoon. The thousands she'd contributed to supporting animal rights, including her very public protest over the disgusting practice of testing 'party pills' on dogs, was immediately forgotten. The decision was made that her right of reply would be limited to a post to her social media page, and that was it — no further comments to be made. The story was set to hit the headlines no matter what we did. And it did, right through to talkback radio. Everyone had an opinion, passionately in support of Annah or furiously against.

In the past protesters had threatened staff and thrown blood at stores selling furs, and two major fashion shows were scheduled that week as part of New Zealand Fashion Week. Safety was a priority. Security was prepped and Fashion Week was to direct all requests for comments back to Annah to keep the lines of communication as narrow as possible and head off a controversy that could be manipulated to sell papers. We just had to sit it out, instead of making further comment that would have prolonged the story and potentially undermined a brand that had been built up over 21 years of tireless work.

That Thursday night Annah had her first fashion show of the week, an event with an *Alice in Wonderland* theme. Over 1000 people showed up in support, including a former New Zealand prime minister. The show was a hit, with rave reviews. On Saturday I flew in to attend the second show, part of the 'Come on Oz, Say I Do' campaign I'd helped create, that saw two lesbian women getting married on the catwalk to help put pressure on the Australian government to grant marriage equality. Of course, the brides wore Annah's gowns. This campaign hit headlines internationally, reaching as far as *Vogue India*. It was a campaign with a social conscience designed to help build the profile of the brand and the cause. The week was fraught with challenges, to say the least.

Now let me be clear: I'm not writing this to debate the ethics surrounding the bearskin rug, or marriage equality for that matter. I'll let you make up your own mind. But what I am demonstrating is that, while each of us has a right to an opinion, when that opinion is made public the potential for a backlash is very real, in which case we must manage our own emotions and go with the flow. Our actions sometimes have unintended consequences, but we can't live in fear and deny ourselves the right to hold an opinion or to make a living based on that opinion — something all thought leaders and agents of influence must do proudly.

Agents of influence stimulate conversations, and it is through these conversations that we incite change, shaping beliefs and opinions that change lives and make a difference in this world. Sounds grandiose, but it's not. You have more impact than you could ever realise. But while we get up the courage to share these opinions, we are not often taught how to deal with the ensuing criticism they can provoke.

Despite all of the media coverage and criticism that Annah received that week, her sales went through the roof, and they continued on an upward trend thereafter. She'd inadvertently polarised her audience and in doing so found a fan base that was now even more loyal to her because they saw through the extremist point of view to the little-recognised work she'd been doing for years.

'Public' enemy number one: how to deal with criticism

Successful agents know that from time to time they will polarise opinions. It's a key to building a massively successful public profile. But how do you deal with an onslaught of criticism that could derail your success (as Annah experienced)? Let's take a look at a strategy to manage the problem.

To reply or not to reply?

The first and most important step when a public attack occurs is to understand where it's coming from. Is your adversary presenting an educated point of view and constructive criticism on a position you have expressed publicly? And do they have your best interests at heart?

If yes to both, and they have posted their critique on social media, allow the debate to unfold for as long as is respectful to all involved.

If the attack is aggressive or threatening, disengage immediately or watch it go viral. In very few cases will you be required to respond, as responding can prolong the attack and open up new wounds, encouraging online flamers to cause further mischief. Take your power back when this occurs. Sites such as Facebook allow you to delete and block vicious comments. Remember, your social media channels are not a democracy. You wouldn't let someone talk smack about you in your own home. Certainly don't allow it online, especially if you're the master of that specific domain. You're responsible for all of the comments on your social media pages, good and bad, and advertising bodies will rule against you if you allow derogatory remarks to remain, against you or anyone else for that matter — even more reason to govern them well.

Understand that the criticism you may be receiving isn't always about you. At times we can all react to certain comments by others based on experiences we've had in the past. Because of these experiences, our responses can be exaggerated and inflamed, especially from the safe remove of a well-lit computer screen. When they are respectful, allow your critics to express their opinions on your social media page.

Debate is healthy and can lead to change.

It can help us to understand all facets of a particular topic and either create a stronger argument or, sometimes, change our minds. But most importantly, understand that...

Just because you have a right of reply, it doesn't mean you should use it

My rule of thumb: don't respond when you're emotional. Ride out the criticism for a few hours, and reply only when you feel you can respond without adding emotion to the mix. Otherwise it's like driving when you're drunk — someone's bound to get hit and it will most likely be you.

Just because someone posts on your social media page, or writes a story about you, does not mean you have to reply, especially if the conversation is going nowhere fast.

If you do decide to reply, first ask yourself what you believe you will gain from it. Nothing, in many cases, other than adding fuel to the fire. But, if you feel you must, and you've removed the emotion from the situation, follow these rules. Always thank them for their opinion and, using the 'what, why, how and why' method shared earlier (see table 4.1, p. 63), identify why you feel the way you do and have taken a certain position.

And finally, don't argue with an idiot, or you'll end up becoming one. You don't have to buy into vicious attacks. This is a no-go zone. Today's story soon becomes yesterday's news. Pick your battles or get consumed by them. Keep your focus on the task at hand. Your goal is to polarise your audience, and if people are expressing opposing points of view it means you're doing your job. Keep up the great work, agent.

'Private' enemy number one: are you thin-skinned?

Believe it or not, it's not what others think about you that matters; it's what *you* think about you that is the real cause for concern. Are you your own biggest hater? Because haters are gonna hate at the end of the day no matter what you do. The greatest gift that we have is our ability to choose our emotions from moment to moment. It's when we allow others to manipulate these feelings that the problem begins.

When you enter a room, I want you to own it. For people to turn heads and acknowledge you've arrived. This isn't about being arrogant; it's about self-worth and knowing you have a right to a place in this world. When you believe in yourself, your perceived value immediately jumps in the eyes of others, and respect is easy to generate. Your energy shifts and becomes massively attractive to all around you. When you don't believe in yourself, others will smell this fear and seek to take advantage when you show weakness. Like attracts like. As pessimistic as this sounds, it is important to be educated and not ignorant, especially in competitive arenas.

I often find myself approached for advice by individuals who are being disrespected at work. I always give them the same answer, and for many it's a tough one to swallow:

The only reason someone has a problem with you, is because you have a problem with you.

Ouch! When we completely and truly accept who we are, others' opinions are like a gust of wind that blows straight past us. We're only momentarily aware of it. It's when we decide to follow this gust of wind into a storm that we prolong our suffering and create even more collateral damage — to our own confidence. You can gain instant relief the moment you accept who you are and all of your flaws. Try it, and watch how your detractors immediately change, without you having to do anything but accept yourself.

This is about becoming thick-skinned and letting go. Over time you'll actually enjoy the 'debate'. Once you accept that criticism is a part of doing business, you allow yourself to get out of your head and back into the present moment, where life is. Don't ever, ever let criticism consume you, because at the end of the day, if it does, it will be your own doing.

Out of every brush with criticism comes a new and evolved version of you.

And it gets easier and easier each time, once you have learned how to perceive it as the opportunity it is. The critics are giving you the gift of evolution.

We all need strategies to mentally respond to others in effective ways, ways that can immediately shift our state of mind and put us in a more productive frame. We can find powerful tools to manage our own emotions when dealing with others, both publicly and privately. Tools that can also dramatically boost our productivity and allow us to make major changes in our lives in positive directions, such as accepting who we are and fleeing 9 to 5. But before we do, we must address the most common cause of failure in this arena...

Impostor crackdown: the top three warning signs

Fears are educated into us, and can, if we wish, be educated out.
— **Karl Augustus Menninger**

Realising your vision starts with your mindset. Our fears can conquer us if we allow them to, especially when we first step out from the shadows that at times can seem as comforting as a warm blanket. Completing the Lifestyle Design Blueprint (see table 2.2, p. 27), introduced in chapter 2, can bring them out in full force. 'What if I'm not good enough? I can't risk leaving my 9 to 5 job! I wouldn't know where to start! I'm struggling as it is! What are other people going to say about me! I'm not an expert, I have no authority to comment on these things!'

This 'stage fright' doesn't just target individuals who are getting started or taking the leap to the next phase in their lives. You're far from alone.

Take Cher, for example. An agent of influence in the field of music who has sold more than 100 million albums and performed in thousands of concerts over a career spanning 40 years. In a great interview on Oprah.com Cher talks about how she still gets terrified before taking to the stage and shares the way she talks herself out of the fear.

Whether you're just getting started or you're well on your way to pro status, you will encounter fears and moments of inadequacy, publicly and privately. Agents know this more than anyone. Why? Because your vision isn't to work a 9 to 5 job; it's to have a real impact and to design your life around your vision — not somebody else's vision of how they believe your life should be.

It's only natural to feel like an impostor at times when you're out there wandering outside of your comfort zone. This is conditioning based on education — education that asserted there is more security in doing what others love than doing what *you* love. To find your 'sequins', as Cher did, you'll need to uncover the three ways to recognise that the 'impostor' in you is set to stop you in your tracks, especially when you're in the early phase of redesigning your life using the templates in the early chapters of this book. These are the three main warning signs:

- You'll doubt you have the 'right' to advise others based on your background and level of experience.
- You'll question your self-worth and ability to deliver.
- You'll sabotage your success by thinking it's not possible.

For now, I want you to recognise any of these fears and self-doubts that apply to you and to momentarily shelve them. Fighting against them is like trying to hold up a brick wall that is eventually, inevitably, going to collapse. By letting it collapse sooner rather than later you give yourself the opportunity to start rebuilding within minutes, rather than weeks, months or years. Most importantly, as I continue to lay out the structure you need to create a business and life that matters, these fears will naturally dissipate.

See beyond right now: focus on the goal before getting lost in the detail

My research into NLP (neurolinguistic programming), popularised by Anthony Robbins, gave me deep insight into coaxing myself out of fear, especially when I was in the process of making great change in my life and jumping the many hurdles I faced. An approach developed by Richard

Bandler and John Grinder in California in the 1970s, it's claimed that NLP can treat problems such as depression, learning disorders, stress and phobias by helping to modify behaviours to support the achievement of specific goals.

I can attest to this. Since I first read about it when I was 21, I've used NLP almost daily to neutralise fear and to help focus myself on my goals. To make my goals magnetic and rid myself of anything that might dull their ability to attract, I found my own 'sequin' technique — a trigger that helps me snap out of an unproductive emotional state. It is a combination of NLP strategies I have learned over the years that helps overcome fears, increases productivity and ends procrastination. It's called *anchoring*.

If you're currently working for another business, you'll know that the business structure provides you with an anchor that gives your life stability — whether or not you love what you're doing right now. When changing paths it's critical that you develop your own anchor that provides you with the emotional structure you need to make the changes you want to make, whether going public with your opinions, being interviewed on live TV, presenting to hundreds from a stage or simply creating your products at home in your own space.

Be the anchor: look within, not without.

Anchors are stimuli that trigger specific states of mind, behaviours and thoughts. For example, something as simple as clicking your fingers can be an anchor that washes waves of emotions over you, from happiness to sadness and everything in between. Creating an anchor means reproducing the stimuli when the preferred emotional state is experienced, so that the preferred state is linked to the anchor. To then release the anchor, all that's needed is to, for instance, click your fingers, touch a knuckle, place your hands together or touch your elbow.

Follow these eight steps to contruct the anchor:

1 Decide on the emotional state you want to experience — for example, a feeling of calmness, connection or confidence.

2 Select an anchor to fire up the preferred state.

3 Think of a time when you experienced this state in the past. What did you see, feel, hear, taste or touch? Let those feelings wash through your body and amplify them, so you feel better and better.

4 Think of a second time when you experienced these same feelings. Amplify them once more. Experience the preferred emotions swirling through and around your body, merging with your senses.

5 Finally, think of a third time when you experienced these same emotions.

6 Feel these feelings rush through you. Amplify them as if you were turning up the volume on one of your favourite songs.

7 When the feelings are at level 10 or higher, release your anchor (click your fingers or whatever).

8 Repeat this step twice more to completely integrate the anchor.

This is the first of two NLP techniques I'll reveal to you to help you find a state of mind that is conducive to fleeing 9 to 5 and doing what you love sooner rather than later.

Releasing your fears around fleeing a 9 to 5 job (which you don't have to do immediately, by the way) and sharing your story or knowledge with the world is the most powerful step you can take to change your life. Create an anchor now, go back and repeat the activity and see just what's possible.

Overcoming rejection

You are limited only by your imagination, and your imagination will turn you into a first-class expert in your field. It's also this anchor that will help you ride out tough situations and overcome rejection, all part of this magnificent process.

Rejected by Ellen DeGeneres

A friend of mine had a contact at Swisse Vitamins, which had recently flown Ellen DeGeneres out to Australia on a massive tour as part of an effort to build its brand. I scored a meeting with the marketing genius behind the campaign to talk to him about Annah's 'C'mon Oz, Say I Do' campaign. I wanted them to sponsor the event and get Ellen to record a message for the new brides that I proposed should be projected on a screen behind the runway.

My idea was rejected by Ellen's producers — for reasons that remain unclear to me. Did my ego take a beating? Nope. I got my foot in the door and secured a meeting. I may not have got the result we wanted, but it did prove to me that you can reach anyone and anywhere if you don't get caught up in what people think of you.

If you're going to get rejected, it may as well be by the best!

Rules of rejection

I once wrote a column in which I solicited dates. I can officially say I was nationally rejected. Well, if you're going to do something, go all out, I say! Rejection is par for the course and it doesn't need to be as all-consuming as many make it out to be. The faster you fail, the sooner you will succeed. Applying the techniques outlined in this chapter, use each rejection, criticism and take-down as a stepping stone to a stronger you. These tools will be handy as you build your profile and meet with new and challenging scenarios. Surround yourself with amazing people with whom you can debrief and share your experiences. It will make all the difference when you hit a major bump in the road, which is inevitable — it's life, after all.

There's a massive difference between pursuing one's goals joyfully and pursuing them forcefully. One way allows your vision to be realised with ease. The other does not. Knowing the difference between the two lies in knowing which way your energy flows, with or against the current. In which direction is your energy flowing now? You can change course anytime you want. You could even do it right this second, if it pleased you.

Tips and resources

→ Polarising opinions is key to building a successful public profile; if people are expressing opposing points of view about your brand, it means you're doing a good job.

→ Don't ever let criticism consume you, but use every brush with negativity as a stepping stone to a stronger, more evolved version of you.

→ It's not what others think about you but what *you* think about you that matters; when you believe in yourself, your perceived value immediately jumps in the eyes of others.

For free tools, tips and techniques, visit www.benangel.com.au /flee-9-5.

10 PLAN IT
The agent's master plan — 100% chance of success

→ The 3D Marketing System to create a plan that inspires you!

The man who moves a mountain begins by carrying away small stones.
— Confucius

'Don't talk to me unless you have a groundbreaking book idea!' boomed the voice over the microphone at the briefing session during the publicity summit. It was Matt Holt, the US publisher for Business at Wiley, one of the largest publishing companies in the world, with offices throughout the US, Canada, Europe, Asia and Australia.

I approached him immediately after being rejected by the producer of *The View*. I hadn't planned to speak to him. In all honesty, he scared the crap out of me. Six foot tall, with a powerful presence, he was intimidating — and I don't consider myself someone who is easily intimidated.

Call it gut instinct, or part of 'becoming a New Yorker', but in that brief moment I quit caring about what other people thought of me, put one foot in front of the other, and confidently walked up to him and made my pitch.

It was over in 20 seconds, and three weeks later I left New York and Hurricane Sandy behind, getting out of JFK Airport just before it was shut down for a second time, this time due to a cold snap that was set to engulf the city that still had much of its power out.

I left unsure of what would come of my testing visit. Opportunities for face time with the likes of Fox News had been wiped out by the hurricane, and I was coming home to a business partnership in tatters. Had it all been a waste of time?

Strike out on your own—it's time . . .

*I was already beginning to realize that the only way to conduct oneself
in a situation where bombs rained down and bullets whizzed past, was
to accept the dangers and all the consequences as calmly as possible.
Fretting and sweating about it all was not going to help.*
— **Roald Dahl**, *Going Solo*

Everyone at some stage has to clear out the old to make room
for the new. And sometimes the universe, God or whatever
you call it, will do it for you. If you're ready to shape the world
we live in and to have greater impact than you ever imagined
possible, regardless of the products or services you sell, the
industry you work in or the message you plan to share, know
that the next step is a critical one. It's decision time. Time to
decide on the tools and resources you will assemble to turn
your vision into reality.

In the previous chapters I've armed you with some powerful
strategies to quickly and effortlessly monetise your message
and potentially reach millions who need your help and
guidance to achieve their own goals. And I've shown you how
to reach them in ways that are meaningful to them and to you,
so you never need to feel like you work another day in your
life—you can instantly flee 9 to 5. But before our journey
ends I want to share with you some strategies that take theory
to reality through your Agent's Master Plan, a plan I've shared
with very few until now.

From theory to reality: will you pass the test?

It's strange how dreams get under your skin and give your heart a test for what's real and what's imaginary.
— Jason Mraz

No matter how idealistic your vision is, it is susceptible to human frailty. Agents of influence are constantly tested and must stay ahead of the game. Let's take a look at the agent of influence's mindset strategies to ensure 100 per cent success, along with one final marketing plan that will help you organise your daily, weekly and monthly calendar based on all the work we've completed together to date.

As we have outlined, *planning* is step 1; *passionately pursuing* is step 2. The two meet and, as in any good marriage, readjust their paths as they travel together. At any given point one may fall off the tracks, and it will be up to the other one to take up the slack until the other comes back online. The best way to stay on track and pass the test is to make decisions — and lots of them, in quick succession. Decisions about when to get started, and about your transition plan if you haven't already begun the process.

Agents know there is no reward without execution and there is no execution without the promise of reward. The reward you gain from sharing your message with the world will be to fulfil your life's purpose and passions. You can choose to amplify your passions or to disempower them by not recognising them. To amplify them and find the courage to pursue them confidently, every night before you go to bed visualise what you want to achieve. Mentally rehearse how things will unfold ... and then let go of the outcome. Great leaders know that for a vision to become reality, they mustn't hold onto it so tightly that it slips right through their fingers. Unfortunately, learning flexibility, going with the flow instead of against it, is an art some will only ever experience in their sleep, when they let go of everything.

Cultivate the leader I know you are by knowing what you want and owning the right to have it, with the understanding that there is no one right path to your destination. Each misstep is also a step in the right direction—you're simply collecting more experiences that are leading towards greater, more profound moments in your life, experiences that groom you for each consecutive step up the ladder, wherever that may take you. It's all on course. You never fall off, you never get it done and you never fail.

Challenge yourself daily by stepping out of your comfort zone and making the decision to ask for what you want.

It wasn't all she believed she would get; it was
all she believed she was worth.

Late one night in Melbourne, after dining out in Chapel Street, I headed for the supermarket. There was a homeless woman sitting outside asking for change. Her sign read: 'Down on luck, please help'. I leant down and asked her, 'Can I get you any food from the supermarket?' She replied, 'Just a banana, please'. A few minutes later I came out with a couple of bags of groceries. I'd bought her several bananas, water and non-perishable items she could put in her backpack.

Driving home I pondered the brief interaction. In life, you generally only ever get what you ask for. Fear prevents us from asking for what we really want. We fear we'll be rejected, laughed at, judged, even condemned. Sometimes we can end up in situations of lack, not because we got unlucky, but because we don't have the courage to own the right to ask for what we want. It's not about being greedy, either. The fact that you're on this planet means you have earned the right to ask; more importantly and rewardingly, you've earned the right to *earn*.

The question is, when did you stop asking for what you wanted?

Inspiration gives us the courage to pursue our passions, while structure gives us the framework to realise them. Blind optimism can impair our judgement, and that's why we must have strategies in place to support our 'asking' for what we want in this lifetime.

Execute it, frame it, empower it: turning a crisis into an opportunity

The Flee 9 to 5 lifestyle is built on experience after experience, and on providing real value to oneself and others. The prospect of retirement makes my skin crawl. Why would I want to retire from a life that fulfils me, is rewarding and takes me to places I never thought I'd ever get to experience? Retirement is a false premise, and while some books encourage retirement, this one doesn't. We need to fill our lives with experiences to bring about personal evolution. Happiness lies in evolving, not remaining in some sort of unchanging lived purgatory. The agent's lifestyle isn't a means to an end. It's about living a meaningful life while contributing to the world at large.

To achieve this, I have one system that frames this entire process from beginning to end. Whether I decide to work seven days or half a day a week is irrelevant. As long as I apply the 3D Marketing System, I've got all of my bases covered, as you will too.

In the previous chapter I shared with you a framework to help support you emotionally. It's now time to frame all of the marketing strategies I've covered in this book within the 3D Marketing System, supporting your business structurally in a way that is designed to generate six- to seven-figure revenues.

The 3D Marketing System: the agent's master plan

> *The Navy is a master plan designed by geniuses for execution by idiots. If you are not an idiot, but find yourself in the Navy, you can only operate well by pretending to be one. All the shortcuts and economies and common-sense changes that your native intelligence suggests to you are mistakes. Learn to quash them. Constantly ask yourself, 'how would I do this if I were a fool?' Throttle down your mind to a crawl. Then you will never go wrong.*
> — **Herman Wouk**, *The Caine Mutiny*

The most successful entrepreneurs and agents have simplified highly complex processes to ensure they achieve their outcomes. They've made them child's play so that anyone can pick them up and apply them — think McDonald's. They have also simplified the steps that they take on a weekly and monthly basis to maximise their time, reach and revenue. These steps and structures support swift decision making, and it's easy to see why: they cut out the clutter and cut to the core of what's important for an agent — building their profile, getting publicity and generating profits.

Whether they know it or not, highly successful and influential agents like Bethenny Frankel, Anthony Robbins, Tim Ferriss, Martha Stewart, Dr Phil and thousands more work within the 3D framework. It's this framework that creates breakthrough moments, makes your life easier and helps ensure success. It helps you plan your day, week, month and year, and within minutes can take you from 'Where shall I start?' to 'When will I start?'

Your 3D Marketing System, also called the Profile, Publicity & Profits Planner, is the control centre for your business. It helps you plan three key projects you will focus on each month to bring in new sales and profits. Using the 'Income-generating activities for this week' worksheet (see figure 10.2, p. 181), you can break these key activities down into weekly tasks to ensure you are constantly implementing strategies that will increase cash flow while building a profitable public profile.

Make it a goal to work on activities in each of these three key areas every week, then watch your business grow while the number of hours you work diminishes. We'll now run through the three dimensions of the system.

1D: Profile—content and collateral

Activities in this area cover everything to do with the creation of content and marketing collateral, and automation that allows you to extend your reach significantly and can be leveraged year after year. This is what turns you into an agent of influence in your field. It's the first step, before you go to market. It's all about planning and preparation.

1D activities include:

- writing articles/guest blogs
- preparing speaking topic ideas that can be marketed to event coordinators
- creating marketing material
- writing press releases
- producing social media updates

- producing products to take to market
- setting up automated email campaigns
- recording educational upsell videos
- project managing or setting up online landing pages
- finetuning your existing marketing messages and then relaunching them.

2D: Publicity — market your message, spread the word

> *There is no such thing as bad publicity except your own obituary.*
> — **Brendan Behan**

In 1D you created content and marketing collateral that will attract your target market. Now you must expose this content and marketing collateral to the world. This is about generating publicity for your content and your personal brand, to engage your tribe. If in 1D you wrote a press release, in 2D you distribute that press release, schedule your social media updates and send out direct email marketing campaigns. 2D is pulling the trigger on your campaigns. It's when you officially go public with engaging content that fills your sales funnel with hot prospects.

2D activities include:

- promoting your free opt-in offer
- running Facebook or Google ads
- running joint or cross-promotional campaigns
- asking for referrals via existing clients

- running ads in other people's e-newsletters
- any of the activities covered in chapter 5.

Which leads us to the final dimension ...

3D: Profits — monetise your message

> *Art is making something out of nothing, and selling it.*
> — **Frank Zappa**

Now, if you've successfully executed 1D and 2D, you should be ready to monetise and profit from your message. Your automated process will have been triggered and your sales will have started ticking over. This is the next phase in your evolution as an agent: increasing sales and profit margins on a weekly basis in big hits.

3D action steps include:

- promoting other people's digital products that are complementary to yours and deriving a commission from them to boost your own profits
- identifying the customers who have already purchased from you, and looking at what other products you could introduce to them (this process returns you to 1D for segments of your fan base — customers you know will purchase from you again. For a dramatic and quick boost in income, tempt them with a pre-order offer, thereby funding your next product launch)

- creating special 'one-off' offers that you can send out to promote specific products for an immediate jump in sales

- launching new products

- speaking at events and selling your products from the stage

- running webinars or Google+ hangouts with an upsell

- pitching for high-level consulting work that takes little time and hassle but is well paid and allows you to continue to grow your online sales with little effort.

Each of these three dimensions is critical to your success. You can't have profits without products and marketing collateral, and you won't get them without publicity and exposure to your target market. Each works in sync with the others. Missing one would be like trying to drive a car without the motor — it's going nowhere fast.

I created the 3D Marketing System through years of testing and measuring, and I've found it by far the most effective strategy for simplifying key activities that need to be done regularly to successfully establish a new agent or to get an existing agent who is experiencing a plateau back in flow. Once you have identified the major projects you will be focusing on, it's time to identify the people and resources you'll need to help you achieve your outcomes. Start now by using the monthly planner shown in figure 10.1 (overleaf) to plan your major projects, then break them down into weekly activities. Your virtual assistant might help you or even project manage the whole process.

Figure 10.1: the 3D Marketing System monthly planner

Project 1: Profile

(e.g. preparing speaking topics; producing articles; creating information products, e-books and so on; designing promotional graphics/marketing material, landing pages, automated email campaigns; finetuning existing marketing messages)

Seven major activities you must do to progress your profile this month:

1 _____

2 _____

3 _____

4 _____

5 _____

6 _____

7 _____

Project 2: Publicity

(e.g. networking; distributing press releases; direct email marketing with opt-in offer to generate new leads via affiliate marketing, joint promotions, cross-promotions, expos, social media marketing, referrals via existing clients)

Seven major activities you must do to distribute your marketing collateral and get publicity for your brand this month:

1 _____

2 _____

3 _____

4 _____

5 _____

6 _____

7 _____

Project 3: Profits

(e.g. upsell or cross-sell other products or services in ascension model to existing clients; special offers to existing clients, telemarket list; book sales appointments; cold calls; ring referrals; tele-seminar; webinar; preview workshops; product launches)

Seven activities you must do to increase your profits this month.

1 _____

2 _____

3 _____

4 _____

5 _____

6 _____

7 _____

People and resources required for successful completion

People I need to contact this month, and resources I require for completion:

_____

_____

_____

(continued)

Figure 10.1: the 3D Marketing System monthly planner *(cont'd)*

Week's priorities

Here are the key activities that I must complete by month's end to ensure I am on track:

_____

_____

_____

_____

_____

Now transfer these activities to the following sheet (see figure 10.2) under the three key areas: *Profile*, *Publicity* and *Profits*. If you find one area doesn't have any activity, re-prioritise to ensure you are focusing on ALL of the vital areas of your business that will grow it the fastest and deliver you income and cash flow sooner.

Now you have identified the major monthly activities for each of these key areas, it's time to break them down into weekly action steps to simplify your marketing and ensure your success. Complete your weekly action plan now using the planner shown in figure 10.2.

Figure 10.2: the 3D Marketing System weekly planner

INCOME-GENERATING ACTIVITIES FOR THIS WEEK

Strategy 1: Profile

Tasks required to build your profile this week:

_____

Date due _____

_____

Date due _____

_____

Date due _____

Strategy 2: Publicity

Tasks required to get your publicity this week:

_____

Date due _____

_____

Date due _____

_____

Date due _____

Strategy 3: Profits

Tasks required to grow your profits this week:

_____

Date due _____

_____

Date due _____

_____

Date due _____

(continued)

Figure 10.2: the 3D Marketing System weekly planner *(cont'd)*

THIS WEEK'S ACHIEVEMENTS

Lead generation

No. of leads desired: _____

No. of leads generated: ____
_____

Source that produced
the most leads this week:
_____

Sales

No. of new clients: _____

Existing customers upsold:
_____

Follow-up calls made:
_____

Avg. conversion rate:
_____%

Publicity

No. of press releases
written: _____

No. sent to media: _____

This week secured media
coverage in: _____
_____

Business development

No. of new joint ventures/
affiliates established:

_____

Number of new speaking
engagements: ____

Number of new business
relationships established:

_____

Marketing campaigns to launch this week: _____
_____.

(e.g. special bonus with purchase; send 50 organisations welcome
email to secure speaking engagements; upsell existing clients
to next program/product in your ascension model; telemarket
database for upcoming event; write and distribute 25 articles to
prweb.com; respond to media enquires via sourcebottle.com.au)

What will I do to launch this campaign this week?

_____

_____

The 20X Formula: if execution is king, distribution is force

There is no learning in the comfort zone and no comfort in the learning zone.
— Dana Eisentein

There is no success without execution, and there are no sales without distribution of marketing materials. The biggest challenge for agents of influence is in lining up their marketing distribution channels to guarantee they have maximum publicity and profits. The 3D Marketing System ensures both goals are successfully achieved by challenging the agent to come up with innovative ways every week to reach their target market by refocusing their thinking.

Time is key here, and there is a clear and distinct link between training and productivity. Writer's block occurs only when there is a lack of structure and knowledge. Overcoming these two gaps has been among the challenges I've shared with you in this book. The product creation system extracts your knowledge, but only constant education can provide you with the inspiration to continue to grow your business and evolve and monetise your knowledge.

It is this education that will help you stay ahead of the curve in trends in your industry, allowing you to claim new ground and harvest the resulting explosion in sales. There is supremacy in habit and habit in self-mastery. All are interlinked. Creating extraordinary results comes from being prepared to do 20 times the work to generate the results you desire. In other words, aim for the moon and you'll fall amongst the stars.

This includes constantly pursuing opportunities to educate yourself, reading, listening to audio books, keeping fit, and keeping your mind healthy and active. At least twice a year, embrace a training course that takes you out of your comfort zone. This will help you find new solutions to the old challenge of creating newsworthy and profitable products, thereby making them easier to promote. Marketing made easy.

Inside or outside of the plane?

A standard 747 can travel at speeds of up to 600 miles per hour (nearly 1000 kilometres per hour). From inside the cabin everything seems to flow as it does on the ground. You are served your meal. You sit back and relax, watch some TV or flick through a magazine, with no physical sense of the speed at which you're travelling.

Now imagine yourself outside, hanging on to one of the wings! It's hurtling along at a massive speed. The rush of air is deafening, it's chaotic, confusing and terrifying. You can hang on for only seconds before your ride comes to an abrupt end and you're flung off straight into freefall, plunging towards the ground.

Same plane. The only difference is your seat on the ride, but the contrast in experience is stark.

Any new journey will have you desperately trying to catch on to its wing to get a ride. After a while you may try to fling the door open so you can take a seat for a while in the economy cabin, before moving up to first class. Eventually you may choose to make the pilot redundant and take full control of your life.

Where are you right now?

Understand and accept that in life each part of this journey is necessary and potentially incredibly fulfilling; it may at times just take hindsight to recognise it.

By finding your anchor you can force your way into the cabin a lot faster than you might have initially anticipated. Once you've got your foot inside, you no longer have to try to keep up with the momentum of life from the outside. You suddenly join it and it's from this position that you can do absolutely anything, because you're finally working 'with' life instead of 'against' it.

There is nothing that kills a career more quickly than the kind of perfectionism that doesn't allow you to get started. Perfectionism in any field is learned and cultivated. In the beginning the road will be a little bit bumpy. Each step you take is building up to an outcome that will change everything. Business renegades and agents know this. Trust the process and understand that in every profession, including an agent's, your role will change significantly along the way. That's the joy of the journey.

Disrupt the norm — and never work another day in your life

Wasting away in life not doing what you love is like drinking a slow-acting poison. There is power in proximity to your passion. Disrupt the norm by dedicating at least an hour each day to what you love doing. The energy created by being close to your passion will give you a launching pad from which you can confidently take off on your next big step up. And, as Marc Anthony said, 'If you do what you love, you'll never work a day in your life'.

If there is uncertainty in your future, *be inspired*, as it means it's wide open for you to choose where that future will take you. In this book I've given you a vehicle to use to achieve it, and it's up to you to drive it wherever you want to go. You've now got the tools; if you haven't already begun, you just have to find the courage to get started.

It finally pays off . . .

The end is not the reward; the path you take, the emotions that course through you as you grasp life — that is the reward.
— **Jamie Magee**, *Embody*

I hit refresh on my inbox. It was an email from Kristen, a publisher at Wiley, but in their Australian office in Melbourne. It was a full month after I'd got back home to Australia. She said her US boss had sent her an email suggesting they meet me. That 20-second pitch in New York led to a contract for the book you hold in your hands.

Had I not been rejected by that producer at *The View*, I would not have published this book. It wasn't even on my radar at the time. It's funny the directions your life will take you sometimes. I don't focus on outcomes any more, I focus on the experiences, the process. That's where I derive my joy. I'm detached from the outcome, and out of that detachment comes great freedom. I really found this freedom only after I was thrown into a situation in which it had been taken away, with only chaos left.

Everything changed after I got back from New York. I overhauled my work practices, including my entire business model. I took back full control of the business. Where there had been three team members, now I had one virtual assistant who contributed 40 hours per month. I was approached by three TV producers and invited to make three appearances in *The Real Housewives of Melbourne*, appearing alongside my good friend the gorgeous Andrea Moss. I took on an international client in the field of fashion, a great love of mine, launched new digital products and redesigned my life from the ground up so I could do what I love *and* make six figures — all in six months.

I downsized everything but increased my profits massively. I had finally learned that you can work less and earn more, with the bonus of operating from anywhere in the world, including Thailand, New Zealand, New York and Australia. You just need the strategies to make it happen — the strategies that I have introduced to you in these pages.

Each of us has a unique store of knowledge, expertise and stories to share with the world. There is no greater gift than knowing that you're influencing opinions, shaping behaviours and empowering others to get what they want out of life, while being rewarded yourself.

You've always been an agent of influence in your own life. What I've shared with you here is simply a blueprint for creating an authentic and amplified version of you that reaches the masses by bringing your unique voice, opinion, stories and ideas to help others solve the problems confronting them. And no matter what your story or message, there is someone who wants to hear it. Incite conversation that inspires change.

Now it's time for you to go out and shape the world. Just promise me you'll begin by shaping your own world. Use this book to create a plan that inspires you, because the plan itself is a source of growth and joy.

My journey wasn't always an easy one, but I can say it has been and continues to be a rewarding one. And the best part is that, just like you, I'm only just getting started ...

Tips and resources

→ Challenge yourself by stepping out of your comfort zone daily.

→ Plan three key projects you will focus on each month to bring in new sales and profits.

→ Make it a goal to work every week on activities in each of the three key areas of the 3D Marketing System — Profile, Publicity and Profits.

Download printable copies of your planner and 3D Marketing System from www.benangel.com.au/flee9-5.

Join me at www.benangel.com.au/flee9-5 for bonus resources, links, and downloadable templates and worksheets for this book.

APPENDIX

Complying with the law!

Most countries around the world have laws to protect consumers (that's you, me and your future customers!) from unscrupulous business practices like false or misleading claims, breaches of privacy and spamming. Each country's laws differ in the detail but the fundamental principles are similar.

While no one expects you to be a lawyer, consumer protection bodies (such as the ACCC in Australia and the FTC in the United States) expect anyone selling to consumers to be familiar with the fundamental principles of consumer protection laws. A similar approach is taken by the bodies that enforce privacy laws and anti-spamming laws. These regulatory bodies have the legal power to investigate and prosecute breaches and they won't hesitate to do so. Fines (sometimes very large fines) are regularly imposed on businesses that do the wrong thing. Attention from these regulators is a hassle and a distraction you don't need. Also, given that information about prosecutions is often made public by regulators, and is sometimes picked up by the mainstream media, it could be very bad for your reputation.

The good news is that the regulators have invested a lot of time and money trying to make basic legal compliance as easy as possible. Their websites (some of which are listed at the end of this section) are excellent sources of information and are written for non-lawyers. Remember also that most laws are built on concepts of fairness, ethics and respect. So while 'legal compliance' sounds intimidating and feels daunting, it really isn't once you invest a little time in understanding a few key concepts.

Here is some information (not legal advice!) about some of the key concepts involved. Make sure you invest some time reading up on the legal rules applicable in your country. I have included some links to various reference sites below.

Consumer protection laws

The golden rule of consumer protection laws is 'don't mislead or deceive'. In essence, this means 'be truthful and accurate'. Fleshed out a little it means don't exaggerate or over-state things, be open, honest and transparent with your customers, don't make things up and don't hide important information in the 'fine print'. Don't make statements you can't back up with facts and don't make promises you can't keep! Easy ... right?

Privacy laws

In this digital age some people are very sensitive about their privacy. Perhaps rightly so! Never before has the potential existed for our personal information to be so easily collected, used and misused.

Not all privacy laws will apply to your business and in fact in Australia there is generally an exemption from compliance for small businesses with a turnover of less than $3 million. But look at it this way:

- Your database of followers is perhaps your most valuable tangible asset (after your content).

- A privacy compliant customer database is a lot more valuable.

- Followers are a lot more loyal if you treat their information with respect.

- Privacy compliance is not very hard.

For these reasons I think it makes sense to aim for basic privacy compliance from the outset. It's also much harder to build compliance in retrospectively later on.

Fundamentally, privacy laws are based on principles of respect and transparency in the handling of someone else's personal information. For example, if you are collecting and using someone's personal information they deserve to be told who you are and why you are collecting it, how you will use it and to whom you will disclose it. Make sure you check out the privacy reference links at the end of this section.

Anti-spamming laws

Spam is sending emails or text messages to people who aren't expecting to receive them. Generally, social media messaging isn't considered spam because people use the platform to choose to follow you. But unsolicited emails or text messages that you send to people directly can be spam — and spam is bad! Not only might you get prosecuted and fined but, I suggest, you will not have a very good reputation as a reputable and credible agent of influence if your communications are perceived as spam!

Generally speaking there are three golden rules to follow to make sure you don't inadvertently engage in spamming:

1 Never send an email or a text message to anyone unless you have their consent to do so. Consent can either be express (for example, a person has opted-in to receive messages from you) or inferred (that is, you have a

business relationship such that it is reasonable they would expect to hear from you). I always aim for express consent as inferred consent can be difficult to establish. Yet another reason why a free opt-in offering is so important!

2 Always identify yourself in your emails and text messages. Give people basic details about who you are, why you are contacting them (for example, because they opted in) and how they may contact you.

3 Always give recipients a free and easy way to discontinue receiving messages from you. This is called an unsubscribe facility. And, if anyone unsubscribes, don't contact them again!

Hopefully this information helps to de-mystify the dark art of legal compliance. It's an important topic to think about and an important aspect to build into your business plan. Not only does it keep you out of trouble but it helps you to be perceived as professional, reputable and competent in the eyes of your followers. What could be more important than that?

Reference links
Consumer protection

www.accc.gov.au/business/advertising-promoting-your-business/false-or-misleading-claims

http://business.ftc.gov/advertising-and-marketing

www.oft.gov.uk/business-advice

http://www.comcom.govt.nz

Privacy

http://www.oaic.gov.au/privacy/about-privacy

http://business.ftc.gov/privacy-and-security/consumer-privacy

http://www.ico.org.uk/for_organisations/data_protection

http://www.privacy.org.nz

Anti-spam

http://www.acma.gov.au/Industry/Marketers/Anti-Spam/Ensuring-you-dont-spam

http://www.fcc.gov/guides/spam-unwanted-text-messages-and-email

http://www.ico.org.uk/for_organisations/privacy_and_electronic_communications

http://www.dia.govt.nz/services-anti-spam-index

INDEX

Index

Learn more with practical advice from our experts

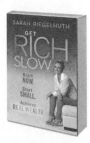